A NARRATIVE

of

SOUTH SCITUATE & NORWELL

1849-1963

A NARRATIVE

of

SOUTH
SCITUATE &
NORWELL

1849-1963

Remembering Its Past and the World Around It

SAMUEL H. OLSON

THE
History
PRESS

Published by The History Press
Charleston, SC 29403
www.historypress.net

All images courtesy of the Norwell Historical Society archives.

On the front cover: The Jacobs grist and saw mills, circa 1830. *Artist unknown.*

First published 2010

ISBN 978.1.5402.2533.7

Olson, Samuel H.
A narrative of South Scituate-Norwell (1849-1963) : remembering its past and the world
around it / Samuel H. Olson.
p. cm.
Includes bibliographical references and index.
ISBN 978.1.5402.2533.7
1. Norwell (Mass.)--History--19th century. 2. Norwell (Mass.)--History--20th century. 3.
Norwell (Mass. : Town)--History--19th century. 4. Norwell (Mass. : Town)--History--20th
century. I. Title.
F74.N98O45 2010
974.4'82--dc22
2010036489

*Pam Kohlberg lived at the "Block House," the John James residence at 45
Block House Lane on the bend in the North River, with her husband and four
children for over a decade, from the early eighties to the midnineties. With a love
of the river and the marshes as an explicit family value, it was an affectionate
compliment for anyone in the family to be called a "River Rat." Trained as an
environmental planner and forester, Pam worked for the Division of Conservation
Services of the Commonwealth as an environmental consultant for the Loring
Jacobs survey and engineering firm and as a board member of the South Shore
Natural Science Center. Although she and her family no longer live in that house
by the river, all share a deep love of the town, its outstanding natural features
and its vivid history. It is a privilege and an honor to be able to support this
publication sponsored by the Norwell Historical Society.*

Scituate Federal Savings Bank is pleased to partner with the Norwell Historical Society on the occasion of its seventy-fifth anniversary. Since 1928, we have been playing an active role in supporting the South Shore community, and we look forward to continuing our long history as a good neighbor to the citizens of Norwell for many more years to come.

Joseph C. Hayes
Chairman and chief executive officer
July 2010

To Wendy Bawabe, president of the Norwell Historical Society, in the organization's seventy-fifth anniversary year.

CONTENTS

PREFACE

The noted historian Barbara Tuchman published a collection of selected essays called *Practicing History* (1981) in which she discusses the craft of researching and writing history. She maintains that the writer of history has a number of duties if he/she wishes to keep the reader reading. She wonders what good is the most scholarly tome that none but the most inveterate historian would read. To paraphrase her: "The first duty is to distil...do the preliminary work for the reader, assemble the information, make sense of it, select the essential, discard the irrelevant...and put the rest together so that it forms a developing dramatic narrative." I have tried to follow these criteria in my researching and writing this narrative of South Scituate/Norwell.

I utilized a wonderful source of anecdotal material in microfilm records of the *Rockland Standard–Plymouth County Advertiser* (1874–1934) and *Rockland Standard–Rockland Independent* (1934–1963). For well over a half century, the publisher/editor of this newspaper and other South Shore newspapers was Frank Stedman Alger who had family roots in Assinippi. In the mid-1950s, he was succeeded by John Bond of Norwell.

It wasn't often that South Scituate/Norwell made the "cut" for a headline or even a front page story—disastrous fires, serious water shortages and efforts at improving infrastructure being exceptions. But it was the short, personal items from various neighborhoods that provided me with nuggets of pure Americana—reports on the thickness of the ice being harvested at Jacobs Pond, the swamp lands yielding a record harvest of blueberries, the gathering of the first mayflowers, neighborly dooryard visits and the number of spring chickens hatched at Tolman's. None of these happenings is exactly earth shattering, but I believe they make up a valuable component of local history.

The following are other salient characteristics of my work:

(1) Given my background in history, I felt I could provide the necessary historical background and interpretation of national and global events and fuse these events with contemporary local happenings.

(2) I focused on the period from 1849 (the "Big Split") down to 1963, when big changes began to occur because of the opening of three direct links to the new Route 3 and the consequent greater accessibility to Boston and the businesses along the Route 128 corridor. Consequently, I was able to offer the perspective that nearly fifty years affords me for the latest events covered.

(3) I decided not to use footnotes or endnotes. One should note that in addition to including an extensive bibliography, I have integrated sources throughout the narrative.

(4) Since many of these chapters were initially written to stand alone, there is some repetition of information to ensure complete understanding of the topic being discussed.

Finally, let me say that to the best of my knowledge, the information between these covers is accurate. If not, I offer my sincere apologies. Also, the inclusion of various topics and individuals, and the exclusion of others, in no way diminishes the importance of those topics and individuals not included in this particular history of the town.

Samuel H. Olson
Norwell, Massachusetts
2010

ACKNOWLEDGEMENTS

First and foremost, I would like to thank our able and energetic Norwell Historical Society president, Wendy Bawabe. Not only did she raise funds for publication, but she also provided a guiding hand in taking responsibility for every step of the process leading to publication. She also organized a cadre of typists, to whom I am indebted, who typed the entire manuscript.

Bill Slattery, our society's archivist, was of invaluable assistance in helping gather photographs and illustrations and preparing them for the publisher.

Others who have my thanks are Matt Gill, editor of the *Norwell Mariner*, who published many of my local history articles over the years. Also, Jeanne Ryer, reference librarian at the Norwell Public Library, provided me with valuable research assistance.

An important force in this effort was a group known as "Project Norwell," of which I was a member and also included Joan Chatfield, Ellen Foley, Pattie Hainer, Alice Hyslop, Tom Hyslop, Bob Norris and Peg Norris. This research and discussion group met frequently several years ago.

Finally, let me thank those, too numerous to name, whose words of encouragement helped me go forward on this endeavor.

PART 1

The Years Surrounding the "Big Split"

1849–1865

CHAPTER 1

LOOKING BACK AT
SOUTH SCITUATE'S FIRST DECADE

THE BIG SPLIT

By 1849, the attempt to keep secret the discovery of gold in the Sacramento River in California had failed, and the entire nation was in the grip of "gold fever."

Tens of thousands were trekking across the plains, mountains and deserts, and thousands of the more affluent were traveling around Cape Horn in the fastest clippers. Both groups were being called forty-niners. Another species of forty-niners were the inhabitants of what had been the southern and western wards of the town of Scituate. After petitioning the general court—which petition included the lines that had been agreed upon by the two sections—both houses of the state legislature assented, and the act of incorporation for the new town of South Scituate was signed by George N. Briggs, governor of the commonwealth, on February 15, 1849.

What led to this peaceable secession that split a town that had existed for 213 years? Norwell historian Joseph Foster Merritt spoke of a town that was spread out over too large a territory and had too many divergent interests: "They, (the inland people) with their bank, their shipyards along the river, their well kept and thrifty farms and heavy pine forests...rather looked askance at the long line of barren beaches and waste land which they were very glad to be rid of."

By today's frame of reference, the reasons why a finite resource such as shore front would be scorned are inexplicable. Merritt also speaks of the town wanting separation for a long time, illustrating the division of the churches with establishment of a second parish near the top of Wilson Hill in 1642, with the main issue being the parent church's belief that only total immersion could wipe out original sin and the inland people feeling that a sprinkling of water was sufficient.

As the occasion of the sesquicentennial of the incorporation of the town approached, a committee of Norwell Historical Society members planned a dramatic reenactment. As they delved into their research, they increasingly felt that perhaps Merritt's explanation didn't go far enough. They asked why the urgency of separation became so compelling in the late thirties and forties. I shall try to summarize their findings for the purposes of this article.

In the waning years of the Jackson administration (1829–1837), the nation was faced with the dilemma of a sizable surplus in revenue. Again, by today's frame of reference, one might ask how this was possible. The answer, at least partially, lies in the fact that the role of the federal government in people's lives was very limited compared to now: maintaining a military, concluding peace treaties, Indian affairs and establishing and maintaining post offices and post roads.

Loco Focos

What use was to be made of this surplus was inextricably tied to the politics of the Jackson era, including the issues of the national bank, paper currency versus hard money and the formation of the Whig (anti-King Andrew) political party. The radical faction within the Democratic Party was known as the "Loco Focos." They were unalterably opposed to the "monster" United States Bank and the use of paper currency. Members of this faction were concentrated in the eastern wards of Scituate. The citizens to the west and south were much more monetarily conservative (pro-national bank) with their sound business practices epitomized by the Scituate Institution for Savings, the direct ancestor of the Scituate Federal Savings Bank.

Congress decided to distribute all but $5 million of the surplus, totaling $37 million to the several states proportionate to their respective populations. Massachusetts's share was $1.8 million, which would be distributed in accordance to the respective populations of the various towns in the commonwealth, with the requirement that the towns use the monies "solely to those public objects of expenditure." The town of Scituate, however, decided to lend the money to individuals, with the inhabitants of the town having preference. From here, the town meeting reconsidered, amended and re-amended, finally deciding that the money "may be loaned to each and every inhabitant of the town."

In 1838, Scituate town treasurer John K. Nash, a resident of the section of the town that was to become South Scituate, felt that the manner of distribution was illegal. Nine years later, Nash's opinion was validated when Scituate authorized its treasurer to call in all notes held by citizens and to use the money to pay off the town's debts. Just a year after this resolution, the split of the town was carried out, with the state requiring that until the results of the federal census of 1850 were in, the new town was still to be considered a part of the old for voting and representation purposes.

Soon the new officials of South Scituate were elected and sworn in. Issues such as financial matters were amicably settled. Pertaining to the dividing of town property, South Scituate got the almshouse (the site of Cushing Center) and the town house. The latter was moved from Sherman's Corner to a location near the present site of the Kent House. By Civil War times, the town house had been moved to the common.

NATIONAL HAPPENINGS DURING SOUTH SCITUATE'S FORMATIVE YEARS

An apt way to describe the mood of the nation in the early 1850s would be to say we were "hurtling along the fast track" toward civil war.

A year previous to our becoming a separate town, the war with Mexico had ended. There had been much opposition to "Mr. Polk's War," particularly in New England. Writer James Russell Lowell's Hosea Bigelow, speaking in a Yankee farmer's dialect, saw it as a Southern plot "to lug more slave states in." Concord's Henry David Thoreau spent a night in the local jail rather than pay his poll tax to support an unjust war.

In 1850, a large portion of the territory we had taken from Mexico—gold-rush-bloated California—was clamoring for admission to the union as a free state. As noted in a subsequent chapter, Senator Henry Clay formulated a compromise package, which he thought, with the support of Daniel Webster, could save the threatened union.

Most Northerners who had been previously apathetic about slavery now became firm abolitionists when asked to support Clay and Webster's concession to the South, which was a strong fugitive slave law. Massachusetts passed a personal liberty law negating the power of federal marshals to hunt

South Scituate acquired the almshouse (located where the Cushing is now) in the separation settlement with Scituate.

down fugitive slaves. Equally effective in increasing the number of opponents to the "peculiar institution" was the publication in 1852 of Harriet Beecher Stowe's *Uncle Tom's Cabin*. Hearts bled over the cruel treatment of benign Uncle Tom by the cruel slave driver, Simon Legree. This was the national climate that prevailed as the new town of South Scituate was launched.

CHAPTER 2

At Work, At School and Other Aspects of Life in the 1850s

A Profile of South Scituate in the 1850s

The federal census of 1850 counted 1,770 residents and 350 dwelling places.

South Scituate contained twenty-one square miles made up of woodland, arable farm land, salt marsh meadows and swamp lands with the North River, a tidal estuary, marking the town's southern boundary.

There were nine school districts and three churches: First Parish on "the Hill," the Universalists at Assinippi and the Methodists (1852) at Church Hill.

There was a town-meeting form of government with four selectmen who were also assessors and overseers of the poor. The first to hold this office were Ebenezer Fogg, Samuel Tolman, Loring Jacobs and Samuel Turner.

There was a school committee composed of Reverend Caleb Stetson, Lemuel Waterman and Perez Turner. There were also nine prudential committee members, one from each of the nine school districts. Anson Robbins was the moderator.

There were two municipal buildings: a town house and an almshouse (poor farm). There was one bank, which was the South Scituate Institution for Savings.

The nearest railroad connections were Cohasset and Hingham.

ASPECTS OF POPULATION

Even the most cursory look at names of South Scituate families at this time reveals that the vast majority was of white, Anglo-Saxon, Protestant background, or "WASPs," to use an acronym coined in the twentieth century. Surnames such as Turner, Merritt, Oakman, Cushing, Sparrell, Vinal, Litchfield, Barstow and Jacobs abound. But a closer look reveals a change was taking place. South Scituate/Norwell was not about to become the heterogeneous ethnic community that exists today, but there was an evolving difference.

The population listing would now include names such as Monahan, Murphy, Dolan and Hines. South Scituate selectmen conducted a local census in 1855, which tabulated the foreign born and their country of origin. In this community of approximately 1,800, there were 74 born outside the United States; 48 of these were born in Ireland, and we can presume that virtually all of these were of the Roman Catholic faith.

The story of the exodus out of Ireland in the 1840s because of a succession of potato crop failures is a well-known and sad chapter in human history. Most came in steerage class at about ten dollars a head in ships that became known as "coffin ships" because of the presence of typhus and subsequent deaths during passage. Since Boston was the nearest port from Ireland, the "Athens of North America" received the greatest number of those coming in the 1840s and the 1850s. An expression of the time was "Next to Heaven is Boston." They tended to settle in East Boston and in the North End, finding jobs as longshoremen and as laborers working on roads, railroads and water and sewer systems in the expanding city. Many of the young women found jobs as maids in the Brahmin homes. At first, few had the resources or even the inclination to move to rural areas since the agricultural life had repeatedly failed them. But NINA ("No Irish Need Apply") signs began appearing everywhere. In 1856, a third political party commonly called the Know-Nothings won all the statewide offices in Massachusetts. They called for restriction of Irish Catholic immigration.

Since many of the more affluent of South Scituate also maintained winter homes in Boston, they began bringing in Irish girls such as Roseann Murphy (Nathaniel Cushing's household), Mary Doyle (Dr. Stetson's), Bridget Curtin (Otis's), Mary Hines (Sylvanus Clapp's), Mary and Margaret O'Brien (Barton Jacobs's). There were also young Irish men coming, possibly to work with the animals in some of the same households. There were several more listed as laborers who had wives and children and established independent households. It is interesting to note some of the spellings in official records indicating either that most were illiterate or that immigration officials or South Scituate officials were unfamiliar with Gaelic names. For instance, Flynn is spelled "Flinn," Luddy "Ludy" and McCarthy "McCartee."

Since most of the Irish were Roman Catholics living in a Yankee stronghold, the closest Catholic churches available to them were in Quincy and Randolph. Most were able to get there only for the most important occasions such as Christmas and Easter and for baptisms, weddings and funerals. But as the number of Irish grew, more parishes were established; for instance, St. Bridget's in Abington (1863), St. Mary's in Scituate (1872) and Holy Family in Rockland (1882). A Catholic cemetery, St. Patrick's in Rockland, was laid out in the 1850s. It is believed that the first Catholic Mass celebrated in South Scituate was in Fogg's Hall in 1887.

The next largest group of foreign born—fifteen—was from England. Two were born in France, and four in Scotland. There was one each came from Germany, South America, Nova Scotia, Denmark and Puerto Rico.

The federal census of 1850 counted thirty-six black males and forty black females residing in town. Many of the blacks—or colored as they were then called—had been here for generations working in the shipyards. Black families tended to cluster in the Wildcat section and in the north end of Bowker Street. William Gould Vinal, speaking of a somewhat later time, maintains there was no prejudice. His boyhood journals speak of the "Grove Street Gang," which included Eddie Winslow, who was black, roaming the

DISTRICT NO. 3.

No. children between 5 and 15, - -	39
Proportion of money, - - -	$199.75
No. scholars in summer, - - -	40
Average attendance, - - - -	27¼
Present at examination, - - -	33
Visitors at examination, - - -	16
Visitors from the district, - - -	7
Wages of teacher, - - - -	$18.00
Length of school, - - - -	5½
No. scholars in winter, - - -	32
Average attendance, - - - -	18⁴⁵⁄₅₂
Present at examination, - - -	19
Wages of teacher, - - - .	$31.75
Length of school, - - - -	2¾

Note the annual salary of teachers in 1855.

woods and swamps of Mount Blue. Both men lived to be well into their nineties and remained good friends. Winslow's daughter, Ruth Winslow Perry, wrote a poem of the friendship between the noted naturalist and the plain-living farmer, mason and fox hunter and called it *Captain Bill and Pa.*

SCHOOL DAYS—"DEAR OLD GOLDEN RULE DAYS"

At the time of the division of the town, there were nine school districts in South Scituate.

The schools were the property of the district in which they were located, and each district was responsible for the upkeep and heating of its schools. In 1838, the state legislature had enacted a law providing for a prudential committee to oversee these matters and to also hire the teacher for the usually ungraded school in its respective district. Unfortunately, the dollar sign, rather than pedagogical skill, was more often the major criterion in hiring teachers.

Horace Mann, the first secretary of the Massachusetts Board of Education, decried the system because it led to such unevenness in the money spent and, consequently, the quality of education in the various districts. Practically all the annual school committee reports in the early days of South Scituate urged the eradication of these committees, which finally did occur in 1866.

There was an elected school committee of three members to oversee the curriculum of the entire town, select the textbooks and evaluate the instruction. Reading the annual reports reveals their conscientiousness in carrying out these tasks. Since there were so many troublesome older boys attending in the winter months—education was adapted to an agricultural society—the hiring of male teachers was favored for the winter term. Hiring males didn't always work out as expected, with the young ladies often receiving better evaluations. The following is one such report for a female teacher: "There is an advantage to employing females, inasmuch as the sensitive, susceptible nature of women is brought to control and guide the earlier stages of a child's progress." On the other hand, following is an evaluation on a young male who had charge of the winter term: "He failed to secure a proper state of subjection and order and resigned as a consequence!" Blame was also placed on an inappropriate attitude on the part of parents, resulting in the district being "ruled by the children." This same report deplored the parents' neglect in not attending end-of-school recitations. For one district, not a single parent came to the closing examination.

The Years Surrounding the "Big Split"

Despite much agitation from 1870 on, South Scituate did not have a public high school until 1888. Those from South Scituate who earlier had received a secondary school education usually attended private academies such as Derby Academy, Hanover Academy and Assinippi Institute. These academies received most of their support from private endowment funds. Mary Louise Nash Power attended Derby Academy before receiving teacher training. Ernest Sparrell, a well-known funeral director and state legislator, had been sent to live with relatives in New Bedford in order to attend a public high school.

Horace Mann's dream was that every child was entitled to a trained teacher. This goal was also echoed by the foremost Unitarian cleric of his day, William Ellery Channing. Unitarians, like their Puritan forebears, placed a high value on education. Channing wrote: "It is a common prejudice, and a most fatal error, to imagine that the most ordinary abilities are competent to the office of teaching the young." As detailed in a subsequent article, Reverend Samuel May left South Scituate, at the request of his close friend Mann, to take the principalship of the first state normal school in America (schools specifically for the training of teachers) at Lexington, Massachusetts. Also, as subsequently noted, shortly after, the first building constructed specifically for a normal school was built in nearby Bridgewater. Many young South Scituate women, graduates of a private academy, attended Bridgewater Normal. Many then returned to teach in the district schools.

In spite of what some would consider glaring deficiencies, most of the graduates there were well served. The scholars—as pupils were then called without regard to the level of studiousness—were firmly grounded in the basics. There was such a din from pupils of all grade levels reciting what they had memorized that these schools were referred to as the "blab" schools. Their textbooks, such as the McGuffey Readers, extolled a strong moral code that emphasized hard work, truthfulness and dutifulness toward parents and their elders. Strong chords of patriotism were also instilled. Words were hyphenated in these readers to stress the phonic method of reading. Noah Webster's blue-backed speller was also an important instructional tool, making a clear distinction between English as written and spoken in the former mother country and an American brand of English with different spellings (center rather than centre; labor rather than labour) and shades of meaning. Englishmen spoke of all kinds of grain as "corn." We called "corn" what they referred to as maize.

All in all, other than consolidating some school districts, there was relatively little change in our rural school system until late in the nineteenth century.

What Town Reports Tell Us About Life in South Scituate in the 1850s

In addition to the very complete accounts from the school committee, the town reports reveal other additional data about life in the new town of South Scituate. The first report appeared in 1850 with William Hall being paid thirty-two dollars for printing four hundred copies for citizen perusal.

Town budgets in the fifties varied by as much as $200.00 or $300.00 per year, usually falling around $4,000.00. School budgets absorbed between $1,700.00 and $2,000.00 yearly with the second-greatest expense being the cost of caring for the indigent and a few insane persons at the almshouse and also for the support of the poor living outside the almshouse. Almshouse expenses were recorded down to the last half penny. Among the costs were bills for supplies from local storekeepers and costs of medical service, heating and clothing materials. For the fiscal year 1854–1855, Dr. A.E. Stetson was paid $25.00 for medical services. An especially poignant entry for the year was $10.00 paid to James Sparrell for two coffins and two shrouds. In 1850, the cost of board for each pauper was calculated to be $0.88 1/2 cents per week. In 1854–1855, the aggregate cost of caring for the outside poor was $77.74. Articles sold out of the almshouse, such as candles, lard, pork, fowl and hay, reduced expenses. They also trimmed expenses by serving town meeting suppers to town officials. The town would also receive reimbursement from neighboring towns to pay for residents of those communities living temporarily in South Scituate and receiving financial aid.

The third-greatest expense in budgets was road and bridge repair, which averaged $500.00 per year. These expenses were cut down by allowing residents to receive tax abatements in exchange for road work. Cost of snow removal would naturally vary from year to year. Snow removal cost in 1854–1855 was $271.33. "Miscellaneous" expenses included cost of postage, stationery and charges of occasional legal fees stemming from litigation with other towns. Also coming under miscellaneous was the cost of small stipends, ranging from $15.00 to $51.00 paid to selectmen and members of the school committee. Names of those paying taxes were listed under headings of West, South and East. There were four categories of taxes: Poll, Real, Personal and School Books. There were 403 poll taxes at $1.50 each paid in 1850. (Note: Even after national women suffrage in 1920, women were not assessed poll taxes. Since most women were not employed outside the home, it would be considered double taxation for husbands.) The aggregate value of real estate in 1850 was $487,366; five years later, the figure had risen to $506,425. Real

Property included "full" houses, "half" houses, outbuildings, shoe shops, orchards, pasture and unimproved land. (Half houses were often referred to as "sad houses," for they indicated either a lack of money or a lack of children.) An example of unimproved land was James Bowker paying a tax of $35.00 on "Hoop Pole Swamp." Personal property taxed included livestock, carriages, bank deposits and navigation tonnage. In 1850, the aggregate value of personal property was $245,816; in 1854–1855, $284,186.

In 1854–1855, the biggest taxpayer in West Ward was Daniel Otis ($204.62); in the South, heirs of Albion Turner ($101.52); and in the East, Jonathan Stetson ($116.37). Each town report contained a list of jurors drawn, always with the stipulation "to be presented to the town for acceptance or revision at the annual March meeting."

Marriages and deaths were not included in the town reports until 1863, and records of birth do not appear until 1869. However, two volumes available for research are *Vital Records for the Town of Scituate to 1850*. Volume I records births and Volume II records marriages and deaths. These volumes were published by the Massachusetts Genealogical Society in 1909.

EARNING A LIVING

By 1849, the glory days of the North River—"The river that launched a thousand ships"—had passed. Years of felling large pines, oaks and larch for ship planks and timbers were depleting the surrounding forests. Also, the river did not have the necessary depth to launch the larger ships that the times demanded. William Delano, known as "Lord North," had built the two largest ships launched on the river, the 464-ton Mount Vernon and the 450-ton Lady Madison early in the century. In the 1850s, his two sons, Benjamin and Edward, were naval contractors at the Brooklyn and Pensacola Naval yards respectively. L. Vernon Briggs's *History of Shipbuilding on the North River* counts only 31 ships launched in the 1850s in the shipyards stretching from Pembroke to the mouth of the river. Compare this to the 170 launched in the first decade of the century, despite President Thomas Jefferson's hated embargo that forbid American ships from leaving port for overseas trade in the latter part of that decade.

The federal census of 1850 recorded that the largest single category of workers in South Scituate was farmers, numbering 147. Second were shoemakers (129); laborers numbered 70, and house wrights (35) and shipwrights (25) followed. There were lesser numbers of mariners, tack makers, trunk makers, wheelwrights and coopers. Those in service areas included physicians, teachers, lawyers, blacksmiths, stage drivers and storekeepers.

Farming was decidedly a more pedestrian calling than shipbuilding, which had been dominant in an earlier era. There were a few large commercial farms such as Henry Turner's Riverdale, a farm of one hundred acres. But most farms consisted of just a few acres accommodating garden patches, woodlot and a hay field. The farmer might also have a horse, a cow, a pigsty and a poultry yard. The big poultry farms South Scituate/Norwell became known for didn't materialize until the next generation. On the small farms, an entire family would work to eke out a living by supplying most of their own basic needs.

Much of the shoemaking was done by setting up a shoe bench in the kitchen or in a small outbuilding. The largest of these outbuildings, one of which may still be seen in a side yard on High Street, were known as "ten footers." A midsized shoe factory, such as Tilden's at the corner of present-day Cross and Winter Streets, and two large factories, Litchfield's on Norwell Avenue and Groce's on High Street, didn't come until after 1870. Some South Scituate shoe workers were traveling by coach to work in the shoe factories of Abington. The old town of Abington then included East Abington (now Rockland) and South Abington (Whitman).

Joseph Foster Merritt's *History of South Scituate/Norwell* contains a very complete listing and description of the many gristmills and saw mills that employed South Scituate workers. Jobs here depended on high water and were, consequently, very seasonal. Among the largest were Bryant's on Second Herring Brook, Stockbridge's at Mount Blue and Jacobs's mill at Assinippi. Another important industry was carried on at Salmond Tack Factory at Church Hill, which was still operating in the 1930s. It was one of the three Norwell sites placed on the National Register of Historic Places, earning the distinction on October 5, 1980. Unfortunately, it has since burned.

Still another industry was the trunk- and box-making factory located on River Street and founded by David Torrey, who had been previously engaged in trunk making for Winship's in Boston. Well-to-do people traveling in those days on ocean voyages or visiting summer resorts in the country required large trunks since quick laundry service was not available. Finally, a unique South Scituate industry was carried on at Tolman's Plane Mill. These wooden planes were highly favored by both carpenters and shipbuilders of the time. The business ended in 1893 with the advent of iron planes.

THE UNION IS DISSOLVED

The impetus toward civil war had speeded up even more by the midfifties. It was the passage of the Kansas–Nebraska Act, authored by Senator Stephen A. Douglas, allowing settlers in the territories the right to determine whether that state would be slave or free (popular sovereignty) that led to the formation of the Republican Party in 1854. The new party's platform did not yet call for the abolition of slavery but only for no further expansion of slavery in the western territories.

In the Dred Scott decision in 1857, the Supreme Court found that Scott, being a noncitizen, had no right to sue for his freedom in a federal court. Further, they ruled that the fact he was suing for his freedom on the basis of having been taken into a territory declared free by the Missouri Compromise of 1820 was moot because Congress had no right to legislate on slavery in any of the territories. From the Illinois prairie came the voice of Abraham Lincoln proclaiming "a House divided cannot stand." In 1858, the senatorial campaign between incumbent Douglas and Republican Lincoln caught the attention of the whole nation as they engaged in seven debates

REPORT

OF THE

OVERSEERS OF THE POOR, OF THE TOWN OF SOUTH SCITUATE,

For the year ending March 1st, 1855.

ALMSHOUSE EXPENSES.

Articles on hand March 1st, 1855.

6 cords oak wood, 36, 2 cords maple wood, 11, -	$47 00
2 1-2 cords birch wood, 10, 11 cords pine do. 40, -	50 00
1-2 ton hard coal, 4.50, 724 lbs. beef, 57.92, - -	62 42
300 lbs. pork, 36, 120 lbs. bacon, 14.40, - - -	50 40
47 lbs. candles, 7.52, 63 lbs. tallow, 6.93, - -	14 45
41 lbs. lard, 4.92, 40 lbs. butter, 9.25, - -	14 17
39 lbs. cheese, 4.29, 15 1-2 lbs. tobacco, 3.56, -	7 85
15 lbs. chocolate, 2.25, 4 lbs. tea, 1.00, - - -	3 25
33 lbs. rice, 1.65, 4 lbs. salæratus, 25c., - -	1 90

Almshouse expenses for 1855.

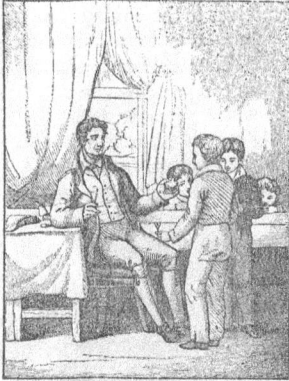

DIVISIONS OF THE GLOBE.

We might have met with many flying fishes in crossing the great Atlantic Ocean, for they are very common in the warmest parts of it.

Quite to the north, and quite to the south of the whole globe of the earth we should find very cold weather. Those parts are called the North and South Poles.

(73)

DIVISIONS OF THE GLOBE.

A typical child's reader of the time, owned by ten-year-old Abial Farrar of Grove Street.

throughout Illinois. Although Lincoln lost the election, he was being touted as a candidate for president in 1860.

The year 1859 saw John Brown's raid on the federal arsenal at Harpers Ferry, Virginia, in an attempt to arm slaves for a revolt. Although Ralph Waldo Emerson saw him as a martyr to the cause of abolition ("He made the gallows as holy as the cross"), others from both North and South viewed him as a cold-blooded murderer.

In 1860, the Democrats split with both Southern and Northern candidates and with another party ignoring the issue of slavery altogether, Republican candidate Lincoln won the election with the required majority of electoral votes but polling only 40 percent of the popular vote. The new decade, despite Lincoln's best efforts, brought the long dreaded war between North and South. In this war, every South Scituate home would be affected. Devotion to the Union and later support for abolition were inspiring despite the many sacrifices that would be required to bring these objectives about.

CHAPTER 3

CURBING THE "DRINK APPETITE"
IN SOUTH SCITUATE

The Reverend Samuel Joseph May, minister of the Second Parish of Scituate (now First Parish of Norwell) from 1836 to 1842, exerted an influence that went far beyond the small congregation he came to serve.

The period from the 1830s through the end of the Civil War (1865) is recognized as one of the greatest eras of reform in all American history.

May's reform interests were multiple: antislavery, public education, better care for the insane, world peace and, by no means least, temperance. His improvident and impractical brother-in-law, Bronson Alcott, whom he had to rescue from dire economic straits from time to time, called him "God's chore boy." His intimate friend, William Lloyd Garrison, the most radical of all the abolitionist editors, christened him the "Happy Warrior." Interestingly, this is the sobriquet young Franklin Delano Roosevelt used to describe Al Smith when he placed his name in nomination for the presidency in 1924 and 1928.

Of all the evils besetting society at the time, many felt "Demon Rum" was one of the worst in that it adversely affected the health and productivity of not only the one afflicted, but also because of the "ripple effect" it had on the lives of the wives and children of drunkards. The Reverend May used children as an instrument of reform in much the same way Charles Dickens (*Oliver Twist*) and T.S. Arthur (author of *Ten Nights in a Barroom and What I Saw There*) did. In this latter novel, often performed on the stage, hearts ached for little Mary as she pleaded with her father outside the swinging door. "Father, dear Father, please come home with me now. The clock in the belfry strikes one."

That the Reverend May loved all children could be attested to by his niece Louisa May Alcott, author of *Little Women*, who loved visiting her Uncle Sam in South Scituate. (Contemporaries referred to our community as South Scituate even before our split from the parent town in 1849.) She had fond memories of sledding on the slopes behind her uncle's parsonage, May Elms. A central part of May's ministry was the Sunday school. In time, he organized his Sunday scholars into the five-hundred-member "Cold Water Army." They paraded around the town accompanied by musicians carrying colorful temperance banners made by their mentor and reciting in unison: "So here we pledge perpetual hate to all that can intoxicate."

After awhile, the pressure exerted by May and his army of children caused five of the six rum dealers in town to close up shop. The lone holdout eventually capitulated, too. A triumphant May loaded his remaining rum supply onto a wagon and drove to a large field near his home, which he called the "Field of Waterloo." Here, cheered on by the children, he swung an ax, splitting open the barrels. Some of the children were so impressed by May's example that they became lifelong total abstainers, even refusing to take the communion wine.

These activities and others, such as the abolition crusade, did not sit well with some members of the community and also the American Unitarian Association. The association suggested the Reverend May confine his efforts to teaching the gospel. Townspeople were particularly incensed when he entertained the abolitionist Grimké sisters of South Carolina at the parsonage. Angelina and Sarah Grimké were unique in that they had seen the degradation of slavery up close because they were daughters of a large slaveholder. It was also considered unbecoming for women to speak in public. The following is a portion of a letter the Reverend May sent to the American Unitarian Association in response to their concerns: "Unitarian principles are fundamental to all individual improvement and to all social reforms. If they wish me personally to omit in my preaching any of the doctrines or precepts of Christ, I cannot act as their agent."

In 1842, May's friend, the noted educator Horace Mann, urged him to succeed to the principalship of the Lexington Normal School, the first school in America devoted to the mission of providing every child with a trained teacher. May took with him as his assistant a South Scituate girl recently graduated from the normal school at Bridgewater. He considered Miss Caroline Tilden to be a genius in the art of teaching.

May's interest in temperance and other reform causes were carried on by a disciple, Reverend William Fish (1865–1885), whom he urged to accept the call to South Scituate. Fish presided over another strong local interest in temperance in the years following the Civil War. The strain of war, including the suffering endured by many veterans from terrible wounds suffered, led to a growing abuse of alcohol. This new antidrinking crusade was spearheaded by many women throughout the country. Mrs. Rutherford B. Hayes, wife of the nineteenth president (1877–1881), refused to serve any intoxicants at White House dinners. She was scorned by many and called "Lemonade Lucy." 1874 was the year the Women's Christian Temperance Union (WCTU) was founded by Frances Willard, with the union using the white ribbon as a symbol of purity. The *Rockland Standard* of June 17, 1876, proclaimed: "The temperance wave touched this town and rolled over it on Thursday evening, June 1." There was a "standing room only" crowd of more than six hundred packed into the Unitarian church. The meeting was addressed by several men. One hundred and fifty people then signed the pledge, and plans were made to form a local reform club. Later that month, the *Standard* announced that proposals had been made for a local women's reform club and a juvenile Templar club.

Within a short time, there were five temperance societies in the village. On November 6, 1876, Miss Emma Malloy spoke at the town house on temperance and also equal rights for women. The organizational skills learned by women in temperance activities were to pay dividends for women as they waged the fight for full legal and civil rights.

The Reverend Samuel May's eleventh commandment, "Thou shalt not drink," came to a theoretical conclusion when American participation in the world war during 1917 and 1918 brought with it a patriotic fervor urging people not to drink alcoholic beverages in order to conserve grain needed

Reverend Samuel Joseph May, the "Happy Warrior."

Enlisting the children
in the crusade against
"Demon Rum."

to provide bread for soldiers, war workers and war orphans in Europe. This patriotic fervor was the catalyst for the very rapid approval of the Eighteenth Amendment to the Constitution (1919). The law enforcing the amendment, the Volstead Act, proved to be unenforceable, a "noble experiment," and repeal of Prohibition came with the Twenty-first Amendment in 1933.

Although Norwell has relaxed many of its injunctions against liquor in recent years, there is still a concern to keep liquor sales well regulated. Undoubtedly, one of the roots of this concern is the crusade of Reverend May and his army of children in the middle years of the nineteenth century.

CHAPTER 4

GOOD NEIGHBOR DAN

The "Godlike Daniel"—"a living lie because no one on earth could be as great as Webster looked."
—According to a contemporary.

After briefly serving as a congressman from New Hampshire, Daniel Webster represented his adopted state ("Massachusetts—There she is. Behold her") for several additional terms. He went on to be a senator from the Bay State for more than twenty years and also occupied the post of secretary of state during two presidential administrations. He had no equal as an advocate before the Supreme Court such as in the Dartmouth College defense. He mesmerized the nation in countless addresses before the Senate and on ceremonial occasions such as the bicentennial of the landing of the Pilgrims and the dedication of the monument at Bunker Hill. He often spoke from memory for two hours. Webster had the ability to put into words what others felt was the tie-in between liberty and union but could not themselves articulate. However, like two of his famous contemporaries, Henry Clay and John C. Calhoun, the prize of the presidency eluded him and went to lesser men.

There is no evidence that Webster ever argued with the devil to save the soul of a South Scituate man (Stephen Vincent Benet's *The Devil and Daniel Webster*), but he was a frequent visitor in town. In 1832, Webster had purchased the Thomas farm of 160 acres in Marshfield, and the "squire of Marshfield" spent as much time there as absence from his duties in Washington would permit. Eventually, Webster had an estate of more than 1,800 acres, where he experimented with a variety of crops, fowl, blooded oxen and other stock. Unfortunately, Webster had two major faults: he constantly spent above his income and had no compunction about receiving monetary retainers from those whose interests he supported in the Senate; the other was an over-fondness for Demon Rum.

The Webster coach was often seen in that part of Scituate that became South Scituate (1849) as he traveled from Boston to Marshfield after concluding his duties in Washington or when returning from the family farm near Franklin, New Hampshire. Each year in the month of September, he had to repair to New Hampshire to seek relief from the catarrh, or hay fever. Marshfield was one of the worst areas of the country for those who were so afflicted. The present Route 53 was the major toll road from Boston to Plymouth and Cape Cod. Coaches leaving Boston at 6 in the morning would arrive at the Half-Way House, also known as Leonard's (located at what is now the intersection of Grove and Washington Streets), at 10 o'clock for a change of horses. The proprietor of the hostelry in Webster's time was Richmond Farrar, who kept twenty to twenty-five horses there. Although a Jacksonian Democrat, Farrar held Whig Webster in high regard. Upon arriving, Webster would immediately want to "wet his whistle." On one occasion, the Godlike Daniel was shut off. It seems the proprietor and most of his staff had gone to a circus in Hingham, leaving a twelve-year-old boy in charge. The young lad had been ordered to serve no drink. Webster called for his usual ration, but the boy stubbornly refused to honor his request. The "Great Expounder had met his Waterloo" Webster sulked, but continued to patronize the facility. He came to admire the boy's integrity and would tip him a quarter for the smallest favor. A few years later, the boy was one of the multitudes who attended Webster's funeral in Marshfield.

Webster also often took the Duxbury stage, which would stop at John Nash's store on the Hill and then link up with the Plymouth stage at the Half-Way House. Nash's son had many fond recollections of accompanying Webster on trout-fishing expeditions. Seth Foster, who in later years owned the house that is now 647 Main Street, was a well-known expressman, running stages to Greenbush, North Marshfield and Hanover. He recalled serving Webster when he would stop at Mr. Nash's store to water his horses and also remembered him as a generous tipper.

An interesting footnote on Proprietor Richmond Farrar came when his obituary appeared on February 26, 1897, in the *Rockland Standard*. Obituaries at this time were not only inclined to be maudlin but also often startlingly candid. The final paragraph of Mr. Farrar's obituary said "he was peculiar in many ways, but he always had a kind word for those he liked. He was always genial and in spite of his peculiarities had many friends who will miss him."

One of Webster's last great services to his country came with his support of Clay's Compromise of 1850. He said "I wish to speak today, not as a Northern man, nor as a Massachusetts man, but as an American. I speak today for the preservation of the union." He knew that if the South were to accept the admission of California to the union as a free state, the North must agree to a stricter fugitive slave law. Seldom has any political figure been subjected to such venomous criticism by a more articulate constituency as was Webster. Emerson, Thoreau, Garrison, Whittier and South Scituate's former pastor, Reverend Samuel May, denounced what they perceived as Webster's infamy. He was compared to Benedict Arnold and Judas Iscariot. But to the average man and woman, not yet militantly antislavery, no words could dull the luster of Webster's reputation. With the perspective that time provides, Webster is now credited with postponing the Civil War for ten years by his support of Clay's compromise measures. During those ten years, the North grew so mightily in population, in industry, in railroad mileage and in grain production, that it was impossible for Southern secession to succeed. Webster would lose his only surviving child in that coming struggle; Colonel Fletcher Webster was killed in the Second Battle of Bull Run in 1862. The Marshfield Grand Army of the Republic post would later be named for the younger Webster.

Daniel Webster died in Marshfield on October 24, 1852. His death was due to a combination of cirrhosis of the liver and a hematoma suffered in a carriage accident the previous May. When citizens heard the tolling of seventy bells, one for each year of his life, they knew their friend and neighbor was gone. Robert Remini, author of a definitive biography of Webster published in1997, includes an interesting footnote on this related to him by Marshfield historian Betty Bates. The bells of the First Baptist Church were not being rung because of disapproval of Webster's drinking habits. However, a ten-year-old boy defied the church's elders, went up to the belfry and set the bells ringing in unison with the others.

The following is a description by Remini of Webster's funeral that was reportedly attended by seventeen thousand people: "Special trains, cars, wagons, and boats, every conveyance that could be had were crowded with people going to Marshfield—a steady stream of humanity. Webster's casket was placed on the lawn beneath a great tree in front of the house so all could get a final look at the great man."

HalfwayHouse, halfway between Boston and Plymouth. Daniel Webster stopped here for liquid refreshment.

There were Norwell people still living in the early part of the twentieth century who remembered the steady din caused by this procession that went on day and night as it passed through the streets of South Scituate going to Marshfield. Possibly there would never again be a political figure that possessed such intelligence and eloquence as Webster; above all, the people of our small hamlet had lost a steadfast friend.

CHAPTER 5

They Answered President Lincoln's Call in the War of the Great Rebellion

1861–1865

The following words are inscribed on the South Scituate/Norwell Civil War Monument: "Liberty and Union Established by Our Fathers; Preserved Unimpaired by the Patriotism of Their Sons."

It is unlikely that few places in Massachusetts—the "Cradle of American Liberty"—contributed as many of its men and boys in the struggle to preserve the American union as the small town of South Scituate. With an 1860 population of fewer than 1,800, 189 men of South Scituate served, with 24 of these making the ultimate sacrifice. This figure is even more remarkable when one looks at a local census taken in 1855 that numbers only 270 males between the ages of eighteen and forty.

Although seven states had already left the Union by the time of Lincoln's inauguration on March 4, 1861, Lincoln addressed the citizens of all thirty-three states in his inaugural address. "You can have no conflict without yourselves being the aggressors." He closed with these noble words: "Though passion may have strained, it must not break our bonds of affection. The mystic chords of memory, stretching from every battlefield and patriot grave…will yet swell the chorus of the Union, when again touched, as surely as they will be, by the better angels of our nature."

A few weeks later, he made the decision to send badly needed supplies to Fort Sumter, a federal fort in Charleston Harbor. On April 12, as supply ships approached, South Carolina bombarded Fort Sumter, and Major Robert Anderson surrendered. Frank Alger, the last survivor of the South Scituate/Norwell Grand Army of the Republic, recalled, on the fiftieth

TO THE
CITIZENS OF
SO. SCITUATE.

So. Scituate needs TEN MEN to complete its Quota under the Call for five hundred thousand men.

Unless this number is obtained before the 5th of September, the Draft will be enforced to supply the deficiency.

We have been unable to get the men elsewhere, and now appeal to our own Citizens to Volunteer and save themselves from a Draft. The following Bounties will be paid to any person who volunteers before the 5th inst.

ONE YEAR'S SERVICE.

United States Bounty. -	$100
State Bounty, - -	240
Town and Subscription, -	300
Government Pay at $16.00 per Month,	192
State Aid-when entitled,-and CLOTHING,	186
	1018

A drafted man gets nothing except the Government Pay and State Aid, thus giving to the Volunteer $590 more than to the drafted man.

☞By Volunteering now, you can have your choice of organizations; whether Cavalry, Infantry or Heavy Artillery; and if desirable, can join any of the new Companies now forming within the State.

With the certainty of a Draft unless this number is raised, we commend the above to your careful consideration.

Sept. 1st, 1864.   Per Order of the Selectmen.

Geo. H. Hamlin, Printer, 120 Hanover Street, Boston.

All South Scituate men were volunteers.

anniversary of the beginning of the war, being in New York City that April when the steamer carrying Major Anderson and his garrison came in from Fort Sumter following its evacuation.

On April 14, 1861, Lincoln called on the states to supply 75,000 militiamen to serve for ninety days to suppress the rebellion. Obviously, the short war that Lincoln hoped for was not to be. It lasted for four full years, resulting in the deaths of 618,000 Americans, out of a population—North and South—of approximately 31 million. The first to answer Lincoln's call for state troops was Governor John Andrew of Massachusetts. Andrew, a resident of Hingham, is recorded as being Lincoln's favorite wartime governor.

The first casualties of the war, four dead and thirty-one wounded, were members of the Massachusetts Sixth Regiment. On April 19, as they marched through Baltimore to connect with the railroad that would take them to Washington, they were attacked by a prosecessionist mob. Other Massachusetts regiments that responded early on in the war were the First, Second, Seventh, Ninth, Tenth and Eleventh. Four South Scituate men served in the First; four in the Second.

Volunteers

For the first several months of the war, there was much enthusiasm for fighting to save the Union.

In fact, the secretary of war had to stem Governor Andrew's enthusiasm as more men were being recruited than the training camps could handle. After the early Union defeat at Bull Run (Manassas), the struggle to capture each other's capital seemed to "bog down." Day after day, the newspapers reported, "All Quiet Along the Potomac." But then came "Tardy George" McClellan's disastrous Peninsular Campaign in the spring of 1862, followed by the bloodiest single day at Antietam Creek (Sharpsburg), Maryland. To encourage enlistment for this war that was rapidly losing its romantic image, the federal, state and even some local governments offered cash bounties.

South Scituate Recruitment at "No Pork Hill"

The town house (town hall) had been moved to the common in 1858. The town house also served as an armory and muster place where military drills were held. It was from the portals of the South Scituate Town House that our men and boys departed for the training camps, with many of them boarding the train at Hingham for Camp Meigs in Reedville, a part of Dedham. The town report of 1863 records the expense of $226.00, and in 1864, $454.52 as recruitment cost. There would be bands playing martial music, speeches, flags and bunting. Still another expense was aid to soldiers' families: $191.00 in 1863 and $136.00 in 1864. State aid for soldiers' families in South Scituate was $3,166.92 in 1862 and $4,650.00 in 1863.

It was during the war that the village area became known as "No Pork Hill"—not a particularly becoming designation for a place where some of South Scituate's more well-to-do maintained their residences. Griping was a favorite pastime among recruits who complained that those serving meals had run out of salt pork to flavor their beans. Since chopped pieces of salt pork were fried and added to beans, chowders and vegetables for flavor, to run out of salt pork was an unpardonable offense, and so the designation stuck for several generations.

Conscription (Draft)

For the first several months of the war, the patriotic pitch was high, but as the casualties mounted, enthusiasm lagged.

Although a draft did not appear to be compatible with the Constitution, Congress enacted the first conscription bill in American history in 1863 as a measure to ensure adequate military strength. The president had always had the authority to draft state militias for nine months' service. Under the new law, each congressional district was assigned a quota. If the number of volunteers didn't rise to the necessary level, a lottery draft would be used to fill the quota. Many of those drafted fled to the West or to Canada; many others were rejected for physical or mental impairment or were exempted as the sole means of support for an indigent parent or orphan. Built into the law was the option of paying $300 for exemption or being able to hire a substitute. In the long run, few men were actually forced into service. Nevertheless, the provision for monetary exemption led to the cry that it was a rich man's war (profiteering) and a poor man's fight. This led to violent protest, the most notable being the draft riots that occurred in New York City in July 1863. South Scituate had no problem in filling its quotas. In December 1862, eighteen men were recruited as aliens to fill the quota. The quotas for South Scituate for February 1, March 14 and July 18, 1864, totaled eighty-five. There was no quota for December inasmuch as the quota for the commonwealth was full.

A War to Free the Slaves

Following the victory at Antietam (September 17, 1862), Lincoln resolved that it was time to do something about slavery.

Many Northerners of abolitionist persuasion had become increasingly annoyed at his inaction on this matter. Early in the war, Mrs. Julia Ward Howe, wife of abolitionist and philanthropist Samuel Gridley Howe of the Perkins Institute for the Blind, was visiting Washington with her husband

and a group of friends, which included Governor Andrew. As she traveled about the city, she visited the encampment of Marshfield's Fletcher Webster's Twelfth Massachusetts Volunteers, which included many avid abolitionists in its ranks. She was so moved by their spirit that that night she awoke in her room at the Willard Hotel and wrote the words of the "Battle Hymn of the Republic" as an anthem for emancipation. "I have seen Him in the watchfires of a hundred circling camps" and "As He died to make men holy, let us die to make men free…His truth is marching on."

With the moral authority given him by Antietam, Lincoln wrote the Emancipation Proclamation, which would go into effect on January 1, 1863. Although he did not free the slaves in the loyal border states, the proclamation brought with it great enthusiasm from the abolitionists and also ensured that England, with its long tradition of antislavery, would not give further support to the Southern war for independence.

THE MASSACHUSETTS FIFTY-FOURTH

Black abolitionist editor Frederick Douglass was among the voices urging Lincoln to allow blacks to fight in a war for their own freedom. Among the first black units was Robert Gould Shaw's Massachusetts Fifty-fourth, a segregated unit commanded by white officers. Six South Scituate blacks served in the Fifty-fourth: Warren Freeman, William Freeman, Benjamin Lee, Jason Prince, Richard Winslow and Henry Winslow. Shaw was among those who died in the assault on Fort Wagner in Charleston. He and nearly half of his regiment were buried in a mass grave. They have achieved immortality, however, with Augustus Saint Gaudens's bas-relief sculpture that was erected on Beacon Hill. In a paper on Norwell history written by Joseph Foster Merritt in 1933, Merritt cites how South Scituate's Edward Southworth, an officer in another black regiment, would have been in grave danger if captured by the Confederates for serving as an officer in a black regiment.

With today's frame of reference, segregating blacks in the armed service doesn't appear very forward-looking. It wasn't until 1948 that President Harry S. Truman issued the order to desegregate the military.

It might also be noted that during the Civil War, white privates were paid thirteen dollars a month while blacks received ten dollars.

South Scituate Men at the Front

It is difficult to adequately summarize the contributions of South Scituate men on the various battlefronts of the war of the great rebellion. Horace Fogg—lawyer, banker and public official—fully recognized the challenges he faced in an address he delivered on Memorial Day 1924. He particularly focused on the Eighteenth Regiment (twenty-seven from South Scituate), the Thirty-ninth (sixteen), the Forty-fifth (thirteen) and the Forty-third (fifteen). Among the engagements the Eighteenth participated in were the Peninsular Campaign, Fredericksburg, Chancellorsville, Gettysburg and Cold Harbor. It was at Cold Harbor (June 1864) that seven thousand Union dead were counted in the first half hour. Charles Gardner of the Eighteenth earned the Medal of Honor for capturing a Confederate battle flag. Only recently, it was realized that there was no marker on his grave in Washington Street Cemetery signifying this great honor. Through the efforts of his descendants and Dorothy Dickson, Norwell Veterans' Agent, and Loring Wadsworth of the Sparrell Funeral Home, the oversight was remedied.

Charles N. Gardner, an almost-forgotten Medal of Honor recipient.

The Thirty-ninth, Forty-fifth and Forty-third were engaged in the final drive (1864–1865) to take Richmond. The casualties in these frontal strikes were so high that General Ulysses Grant was often called "Butcher."

Frank Alger, South Scituate's last survivor, was able in later years to return to many of the places he had been during the war. He had been severely wounded in the Union defeat at Olustee, Florida, and was left for dead on the field. In fact, the captain of his company had written his parents informing them of his death. He had been picked up by the Confederates and sent to Andersonville Prison in Georgia, where his weight dropped from 165 to 90 pounds. Subsequently, he was sent to rebel prisons at Charleston and Florence, South Carolina. He was at Florence when David Willard Robinson, age eighteen, died. David, for whom the South Scituate Grand Army post was named, served with his father, David P., in Company H, Second Massachusetts. They too had been at Andersonville and were later moved to Florence. Months of the severest privation had taken their toll and young Robinson died while lying under the same blanket as his father. Refused permission to bury his boy, the father's last sight of his son was when he placed the remnant of his handkerchief over the face of his dead son prior to his burial.

THE NAVAL WAR

The naval aspects of the war, though important, paled in comparison to the significance of the land war. Twenty-two men from South Scituate saw naval service. The major role of the navy was maintaining a tight blockade of the Confederate coastline. It was the advent of the iron ships that further ensured Northern maintenance of the blockade. One South Scituate man at the center of things was the individual for whom the Norwell Camp of the Sons of Union Veterans was named. Frederick H. Curtis was serving on the gunboat *Congress* when it was rammed by the *Merrimac*, which was actually a Northern merchant ship that had been captured by the South and renamed the *Virginia*. Young Curtis refused to surrender and swam three-quarters of a mile to shore. The next day, Curtis witnessed from a treetop the epochal fight between the *Merrimac* and the Union ironclad, the *Monitor*. At his death, the *Boston Journal* eulogized Curtis as the "fighting edge" of the true Yankee sailor.

Finally, no account of South Scituate's role in the war on the sea would be complete without including the names of the Delano brothers, Benjamin and Edward. Benjamin, as chief naval constructor at Brooklyn, oversaw

Frederick H. Curtis, the "fighting edge" of the true Yankee sailor, according to the *Boston Journal*.

the conversion of numerous merchant ships to war purposes and also constructed twenty-one battleships. Although Edward had died two years before the war began, he had served as naval constructor at Pensacola, Norfolk and Charleston. He was responsible for building Admiral Farragut's flagship, the *Hartford*.

CHAPTER 6

TRAGEDY, DEFEAT AND
THE ULTIMATE TRIUMPH

IN HIS OWN WORDS

By the time of the Civil War, photography had made great strides from the time of the first daguerreotypes, a scant twenty-five years before.

The battles are well documented with graphic photos by Alexander Gardner and Matthew Brady. Officers aspiring to become the new Napoleon sat for the cameras in their fastidious uniforms in the Napoleonic pose of holding one hand inside their tunics. More haunting are photographs of young men, some barely out of their teens, staring straight ahead into the camera to ensure that their families had their likeness in the event they might meet death on some Southern battlefield or, less gloriously, die in a field hospital from some infectious disease such as measles, smallpox or dysentery, which often swept uncontrollably through the army encampments. One such photograph is that of eighteen-year-old Abial Farrar, a Back Streeter (Grove) who resided in the house later occupied by Professor William Gould Vinal. "Cap'n Bill" possessed several letters pertaining to Abial Farrar's army stint, and his family allowed the Norwell Historical Society to copy these letters for their archives.

An early letter written to his sister describes the sea voyage and arrival at Fortress Monroe in Virginia. With perhaps some bravado, he writes: "I like it here first rate so far. I think I'd rather be out here than shoe-making, but perhaps I shant after I've seen a fight or two."

Further letters describe the monotony of picket duty and construction of breastworks (precursor of the trenches of World War I) for the coming siege of Petersburg. Another letter relates activities reminiscent of Sherman's campaign in Georgia with his description of burning and twisting rails (Sherman's "hairpins") and destroying farm crops and livestock—doing everything possible to prevent the Confederacy from continuing the war at one level or another. He describes raiding parties on civilian property when some of the boys stole gold watches and raided cellars with stores of butter, molasses and all kinds of preserves, which provided welcome variation of a soldier's usual ration of coffee and worm-infested hard tack. He tells of marching through incessant rain and sloughing through mud a foot deep that quickly froze as thick as brick. The privation endured resulted in his being sent to "sick bay" and writing letters home with the logo of the Sanitary Commission (forerunner of the Red Cross). He's grateful for the commission's gifts of paper, pens, lead pencils, shirts, stockings and all kinds of Jell-O for the very sick ones. In these letters, he asks his mother to send him gift boxes filled with all the things he likes, such as apples and shortcakes. He tells his home folks of a visit from Oliver Prouty, another young soldier from South Scituate.

Toward the end of February 1865, his condition worsened, and he was sent to the army hospital at City Point, Virginia. His letters then voice complaints about his growing weakness and continued trouble with what he called the "diareer." One could surmise that this condition causing dehydration—a matter treatable today—was the cause of his death on March 4, 1865. In his last letter, the handwriting isn't as firm and he signs off: "I think this will do for this time so goodbye from your son, Abial Farrar."

The final communication in the packet is a telegram to Mr. Farrar from City Point dated January 9, 1866, informing Abial's father that, in accord with his request, the remains of his son will be sent back to South Scituate. The regimental officer also promises that he will contact the family on his return home. He informs the family that the headboard (temporary grave marker) is in the outside case, and that the temporary grave had been enclosed and had not been disturbed.

One of the most heart-rending songs from the Civil War obviously would have had special meaning for the Farrars as it did for the countless other families, North and South. A portion of it is included here. The words are by Henry Washburn, and the lyrics by George Root.

Abial Farrar was only eighteen when he gave "the last full measure of devotion," as Abraham Lincoln referred to in his Gettysburg Address.

"The Empty Chair"

We shall meet,
But we shall miss him
There will be one vacant chair
We shall linger to caress him
While we breathe
Our evening prayer;
When a year ago we gathered
Joy was in mild blue eye,
But a golden chord is severed
And our hopes in ruin lie.

Chorus:
We shall meet,
But we shall miss him
There will be one vacant chair
We shall linger to caress him
While we breathe
Our evening prayer.

THE HOME FRONT

The major impact of the war on South Scituate was, considering its small size, the very large number of fathers, sons and brothers who served—considerably more than half of those of military age—and the ever-present fear that a loved one might never return home. A secondary impact was the high level of prosperity engendered by the war. Agricultural production and demand soared. Local sawmills, box factories and tack factories flourished. By Civil War times, much of the shoemaking had shifted from small home workshops to factories, although local shoe factories such as Litchfield's and Groce's didn't come until the decade following the war. South Scituate shoe workers found jobs in the factories of Abington that then included East Abington (Rockland) and South Abington (Whitman). Abington and North Bridgewater (Brockton) together produced a very large percentage of the boots and shoes worn by the Union army. If workers left for the army, they were quickly replaced by immigrants who, despite the war, were pouring into the country.

Local churches prepared boxes full of useful items for the soldiers, and women and girls met regularly in the town house and in the churches making bandages and knitting socks, scarves and so forth. There is no record of South Scituate girls joining Miss Dorothea Dix's Nursing Corps, but authoress Louisa May Alcott, niece of Reverend Samuel May and frequent visitor to South Scituate in her childhood, did and left an account of her work in wartime Washington in a book titled *Hospital Sketches.*

ANNUS MIRABILIS, 1863

One of the rare times that the Confederate army engaged the Union army on northern soil was in the three-day battle of Gettysburg on July 1 through July 3, 1863. The climax came on the third day, when Confederate general

George Pickett's charge against Cemetery Ridge was halted by superior artillery, and General Robert E. Lee's Army of Northern Virginia retreated from Pennsylvania. Charles W. Reed, the noted artist who lived in West Norwell later in his life, received the Medal of Honor for his heroic action at Gettysburg, on July 2, 1863, saving the life of his captain, John Bigelow. Reed is also remembered for his sketches of Civil War camp life titled *Hardtack and Coffee*, which appeared in Frank Leslie's *Illustrated*.

An additional reason for rejoicing came on July 4, 1863, with the news that Vicksburg, the last Confederate stronghold on the Mississippi, had fallen, thus splitting the Confederacy in half. Lincoln summed up the importance of this victory by saying, "The 'Father of the Waters' now runs by unvexed to the sea."

That November, Lincoln agreed to go to Gettysburg and say a few words at the dedication of the soldiers' cemetery. Senator Edward Everett of Massachusetts, the orator of the day, admitted that Lincoln had better caught the full meaning of the war with his "few words" than he had in a two-hour oration. Lincoln forecast that despite the awful carnage here and elsewhere that "this nation under God will have a new birth of freedom."

Thanksgiving had been quite frequently observed, particularly in New England, ever since the first one at Plymouth in 1621, but the first nationally observed one didn't come until this "year of wonders." Mrs. Sarah Josepha Hale, editor of Godey's *Ladies Book* and author of "Mary Had a Little Lamb," visited Lincoln and urged him to proclaim a national day of thanksgiving in view of the military successes of that year and the bountiful harvests reaped despite the war. Lincoln proclaimed the last Thursday in November as Thanksgiving, which has been observed nationwide ever since. In 1939, traditionalists were outraged when President Franklin D. Roosevelt proclaimed the third Thursday, and it went back to the traditional day thereafter.

Among New Englanders during Civil War times, with a lingering attitude that Christmas celebrations smacked of popery, Thanksgiving exceeded December 25 in importance.

DOMESTIC ACHIEVEMENTS OF THE LINCOLN ADMINISTRATION

The Civil War years yielded several pieces of landmark legislation. Among them were legislation for building the transcontinental railroad, the Homestead Act, the creation of the Department of Agriculture, the National Banking Act and the Morrill Land Grant Act. The Morrill Land Grant Act provided public land in the West to states in accordance to their size, which then could be sold with the revenue used to endow colleges specializing in agriculture and the mechanical arts.

Massachusetts was awarded 340,000 acres. Thus, the Massachusetts State College came into being, derided by some as a "cow college" or as "Mass Aggie." A young man from South Scituate, William Penn Brooks, was one of the first to avail himself of this opportunity to attain an inexpensive college education. One small piece of the Brooks's land on Main Street was the farm operated until quite recently by the Osborne family. After graduation, Professor Brooks taught for many years at his alma mater, the forerunner of the University of Massachusetts. In the early years of the twentieth century, he taught agriculture at a number of Japanese universities. Professor Brooks always credited the South Scituate farm on which he grew up as being the foundation of all he knew.

The War Draws to a Close

Despite the military successes of 1863, late 1864 and 1865 brought mounting casualties as Grant fought relentlessly on the line before Richmond. Lincoln expected to be defeated by Democratic challenger George B. McClellan in the election of 1864. But that fall, General Sherman captured Atlanta and began his march across Georgia to the sea, a feat Lincoln modestly credited for his re-election. The following April, Grant finally took Richmond, and a few days later he met Lee in a farmhouse at Appomattox Court House in Virginia to discuss surrender terms. Grant's show of magnanimity to a formidable foe proved to be his finest hour.

On March 4, 1865, Lincoln had been sworn in for a second term promising a nonvindictive peace, "with malice toward none, with charity for all." That an assassin's bullet prevented him from carrying this out was a tragedy for the South and led to what has been called the "Crime of Reconstruction."

Aftermath and Reconciliation

South Scituate veterans returned to their homeplaces and were honored for the rest of their lives for their noble service. For most of them, the war remained the great adventure of their lives. On December 21, 1865, in a ceremony held in the State House presided over by John Andrew, the returning regimental flags were placed in Memorial Hall, later to be called the "Hall of Flags," as the final act in the war of the great rebellion.

The Years Surrounding the "Big Split"

The rancor brought on by the war was put aside less easily. But it was a grand gesture when several Confederate generals marched in General Grant's funeral procession in 1885.

A local gesture of reconciliation came twenty-one years later. In 1906, seventy-eight-year-old lifelong bachelor Benjamin Prouty announced his impending marriage. Prouty, who had served with the Massachusetts Thirty-ninth for two years, had met his intended through correspondence. In one letter, he had described himself as a "crippled old man, without any teeth, and pretty well used up." His bride was Miss Lucretia Early, a niece of Confederate general Jubal Early. The marriage lasted only six months with Mr. Prouty dying in April 1907. Neighbors testified that during his final illness, Mrs. Prouty had nursed him with the tenderness of a child.

Possibly Norwell's last direct line to the Civil War came in 1950 with the death of Mrs. Sarah Maynard at the great age of ninety-seven. Born to a slave family in Fredericksburg, Virginia, she had vivid memories of the 1862 battle. Toward the close of her life, this child of the Confederacy would receive special recognition from Norwell veteran organizations who would visit her home on Pine Street with gifts of flowers on each Memorial Day.

PART 2

From the Close
of the Civil War to the
Turn of the Century

CHAPTER 7

THE ORIGINS OF NORWELL'S
CIVIL WAR MONUMENT

Standing on the South Scituate/Norwell Common for the last 127 years is an imposing spire of New Brunswick granite of a highly polished red color. Inscribed on it are the names of twenty-four soldiers and sailors of South Scituate who fought and died for liberty and the Union during the years of the Civil War, from 1861 to 1865. These names represent an impressive sacrifice for a village, which at the time had fewer than 1,800 inhabitants. Thirteen years of community effort were required before a fitting memorial for these men, who in Lincoln's words gave their "last full measure of devotion," was dedicated on July 3, 1878, the fifteenth anniversary of the Union victories at Gettysburg and Vicksburg.

The Grand Army of the Republic (GAR), an organization of Union veterans, was founded in 1866. Among its objectives was a commitment to foster the camaraderie and sacrifice that bonded the "band of brothers" that represented every social strata, including black men. The General Charles Griffin Post no. 112 of South Scituate was chartered November 25, 1869, with ten charter members enrolled. In 1871, the post was renamed to honor South Scituate youth D. Willard Robinson, who had died in the Confederate prison at Florence, South Carolina. A perusal of the post's official journal, now housed in the archives of the Norwell Historical Society, indicates an increasing urgency to properly honor its fallen comrades. But the 1870s were a time of economic downturn, both nationally and locally. In fact, many local GAR members let their membership lapse because the yearly dues of $4.00 were difficult to come by. The memorial effort had its inception in

May 1871 when the post appointed a committee of one individual from each school district to solicit funds for the proposed monument; $161.50 was thus realized. The Ladies Aid Society gave unexpended money from the treasury, amounting to $83.21. A course of lectures given in October brought another $75.00. Before ground could be broken for a base, interested persons met in the town hall to determine a site. A central question that was raised was: who owned the land on the common? Permission to locate was thus granted by the corporations of both the First Parish and the town.

But progress again lagged during the mid-1870s as hard times deepened. Fortunately, the effort gained steam in September 1877, when the ladies of the town conducted a three-day fair at which the Honorable John Long, later a Massachusetts governor and U.S. secretary of the navy, was the main speaker. This effort brought $300.00. Since the projected cost of the base had escalated due to delays, the post in 1878 asked the town to appropriate $1,000.00 to complete the job; the town acceded to this. The committee appointed to complete the task managed to cut costs further by purchasing a completed spire that a New Hampshire town had ordered but for some reason did not use. The total cost of the foundation, base and monument was $1,719.50. A number of items were placed under the base: names of Post no. 112 comrades, rules and regulations of the GAR and voting records of both the First Parish and the town for locating the monument.

July 3, 1878, was a scorching day that, nevertheless, proved to be one of the most impressive and memorable in the history of the town. Citizens throughout the town decorated their homes and businesses with flags and banners. Members from seven neighboring posts were in the first divisions of the parade. Several civic groups, Masonic lodges and temperance groups, such as the Women's Christian Temperance Union, made up the second division. The third division was composed of school children and other townspeople.

General Horace Sergeant Binney, commander of the Massachusetts GAR, was the principal orator. He and other dignitaries were escorted to the home of Ebenezer Fogg, now the Freeman residence, where they were entertained. At 11:30 a.m., the posts marched to town hall, which was then situated where the Kent House is now located, where a bountiful collation had been spread. After GAR members were served, about five hundred of the general public partook of the delicacies.

Miss Carrie Simmons, daughter of one of the memorialized soldiers, unveiled the monument. Since the day was so hot, the speaking part of the event continued in the Unitarian Church. Because of the resultant delays, the main orator of the day was unable to finish his speech as he and his attendants had to be rushed to Greenbush to catch the last train for Boston. Also marring the day, according to the Rockland's *Standard* newspaper, was the presence of many pickpockets. One unlucky individual was relieved that afternoon of his gold watch.

In 1868, GAR commander in chief John Logan had issued General Order no. 11, calling for all posts to remember their fallen comrades by decorating their graves on May 30. Soon May 30, officially Memorial Day, was generally referred to as "Decoration Day." In addition to decorating veterans' graves on that day, there would be parades and ceremonies at the monument. There would be addresses by public officials, and the school children, who revered the "boys in blue," would recite patriotic pieces. In these years, during which time South Scituate changed its name to Norwell, town appropriations as large as one hundred dollars—a large sum for that time—would be made to help defray expenses for the day. For many years, the South Scituate Brass Band would provide the music. As the ranks of the GAR thinned, Norwell veterans of the world war picked up the functions of the GAR through their membership in the American Legion. In the early

South Scituate's memorial to its twenty-four Civil War dead.

Right: A striking monument of New Brunswick granite.

Below: Dedication Ceremony on July 3, 1878.

PROGRAMME OF EXERCISES

———— AT THE ————

MONUMENT.

———

Unveiling the Monument,   *With appropriate Music by the Band.*

Prayer, ...   *By Chaplain of the Day.*

Remarks,   .   .   .   *By President of the Day.*

MUSIC BY THE BAND.

Presentation and Delivery of the Monument.

Reception of the Monument.

MUSIC BY THE BAND.

Oration,   .   .   .   *By Gen. Horace Binney Sargent.*

MUSIC BY THE BAND.

Benediction.

FIRST DIVISION.

ALPHEUS THOMAS, *Chief of Division.   Aids.*

This Division will consist of the following Posts of the G. A. R.
Nos. 58, 74, 83, 104, 111, 127, 31.

———

SECOND DIVISION.

E. T. VINAL, *Chief of Division.   Aids.*

This Division will consist of Masonic, Odd Fellows and Temperance Lodges, Temple of Honor, Divisions of S. of T., Reform Clubs, and the Woman's Christian Temperance Union.

———

THIRD DIVISION.

J. H. CURTIS, *Chief of Division.   Aids.*

This Division will consist of the Children from the several Schools, Citizens of the Town, and all other persons who desire to march in the procession.

The Posts of the G. A. R. are requested to report at the Town Hall at 9 o'clock.

The several Divisions will form promptly at 1 o'clock, as follows: First Division on Main Street, right resting on West Street; Second Division on Central Street, right resting on Main Street; Third Division on Main Street, right resting on River Street.

The escort will form at the Town Hall at 12:45. and march to the "James Library Building," receive the Orator, Chaplain, and President of the Day, and invited guests.   At 1:15 the escort will move, receiving each Division in order into the procession,—pass through River, Dover and Main Streets to the junction of Lincoln Street, countermarch by Main, West and River Streets to the Common.

South Scituate men sign the official journal of D. Willard Robinson Post no. 112, Grand Army of the Republic (GAR).

1920s, a memorial boulder listing the names of all veterans of this latter war was placed on the common.

A few years ago, Norwell's tradition of honoring the sacrifices of its young men and young women was continued when a granite wall containing the names of all who served in World War II, Korea and Vietnam was placed nearby. The South Scituate/Norwell Veterans Memorial Common was now complete.

CHAPTER 8

A GOLDEN AGE OF
LOCAL PHILANTHROPY

The residents of South Scituate/Norwell have benefited through the years by the generosity of many who have lived among us. A most notable example in more recent times is the gift by Eleanor Norris of 117 acres in memory of her husband, Albert F. Norris; the property is now managed by the Trustees of Reservations. In reviewing the history of the town, the waning years of the nineteenth century stand out as another banner era of generosity benefiting the townspeople.

The time between 1870 and the turn of the last century is often referred to as the Gilded Age, taken from the title of a novel by Mark Twain and Charles Dudley Warner that chronicled the lives of the nouveaux riches and their lack of genuine values, particularly the flaunting of their wealth in garish ways. Charles Francis Adams Jr. remarked that he wouldn't care to meet any of these newly minted millionaires "either in this world or in the next." Commenting on the times, another observer declared that the man in the moon had to hold his nose when passing over planet Earth. Many of the politicos of the times allied themselves with the titans of the era for their mutual advantage. South Scituate/Norwell then had a number of people who, according to the standards of the time, possessed considerable assets, acquired either through their own efforts or by inheritance.

Despite these means, most of the local wealthy, many of them summer people, tended to live in a relatively modest style. Moreover, many used a portion of their money to make this small rural community a better place for all its citizens.

The James Library is once again a "Painted Lady" of the Victorian era.

The genesis of the James Library came in 1865, the first year of the ministry of Reverend William Fish. While the Reverend Fish and his wife were keeping a private school in Illinois, they formed a friendship with Josiah Leavitt James, whose wife was a sister of Reverend Samuel Deane, pastor of Second Parish of Scituate from 1810 to 1834. Before moving to Illinois in 1834, where he founded a new town called Trimont, James had been a partner of John Nash, who kept a store on the Hill. In 1865, James learned from his niece, Hannah Packard James, of efforts to replenish the Sunday school library. He responded with a check for $1,000 to be invested with its income being used for the purchase of books. When the members of the church began thinking about the building's library, Mr. James sent another $1,000 for that purpose, providing that the parish would match his gift. This was agreed to. Mr. Israel Nash then gave a lot valued at $1,300 as a site. Other gifts began to pour in with Miss Abigail Otis also leading the way with $1,000. A public subscription drive in 1873 netted $13,515, with Nathan Cushing, Mrs. Hannah Merritt Norwell, Miss Prudence Delano and Benjamin Delano, formerly the naval contractor at Portsmouth and Brooklyn, among the substantial donors. Over the years, Mr. James donated $5,920.

The library, designed by William Sparrell, was in the Italianate style modified by the use of Queen Anne-style windows. It was built by Leander Sherman of North Marshfield, and its dedication was held on May 1, 1874.

The library is administered solely by First Parish and relies on several annuities and private contributions for its existence. When William Nash

From the Close of the Civil War to the Turn of the Century

of Arlington, formerly of South Scituate, died in 1880, he left $1,000 for its enlargement.

In 1902, the James became a free public library for all the townspeople, even though still owned by First Parish and operated by the trustees. In 1911, the town first appropriated $100 for the library, which was increased to $200 per annum in 1934. The last town appropriation, $14,000, was made in 1973, just before the opening of the Norwell Public Library.

The James has served the town admirably for a century and a quarter. It's been used as a meeting place for groups such as the Young People's Christian Society, the Boy Scouts and the Norwell Historical Society.

A new lease on life came when the building once again became a "Painted Lady," using the earth colors popular in the Victorian age. In 1994, it became the Center of the Arts in Norwell with regular Sunday concerts and teas, literary discussion groups and an exhibit area for regional artists.

The First Parish Church, built for $4,650 in 1830, underwent extensive renovations in 1878, which was made possible by generous subscribers. Among the improvements were frescoed wall treatment, wall sconces fueled by kerosene, which replaced the original sperm oil lamps, and colored glass windows.

In 1887, William and Julianna Sparrell gave the clock in the steeple in memory of their father, who was architect of the 1830 structure. In that same year, Miss Abigail Otis provided the recast Revere bell in the belfry. It was said that self-interest was a factor in her gift in that she wanted to hear the bell more distinctly when it struck the hours.

First Parish's history of rotating parsonages ended when the Pickles Cushing place, now numbered 644 Main Street, was obtained and renovated

The Second Parish of Scituate (now First Parish of Norwell) was the fifth meetinghouse built in 1830 during the ministry of Reverend Samuel Deane.

61

largely through the generosity of Miss Otis. As a condition of her gift, she insisted that Reverend Fish have a lifetime lease on the manse.

The community's best-known benefactor of the time was the man responsible for Norwell being the only town in the entire country having that name. Henry Norwell was not a native of the town, having been born in Scotland in 1832. Henry Norwell's rise was a true-life Horatio Alger success story. At the age of fourteen, he was apprenticed to a dry-goods merchant in Limerick, Ireland. Coming to America in 1855 in the first of ninety-eight trans-Atlantic crossings made in his lifetime, he lived in Illinois for a time and then came to Boston where he found employment with a dry-goods firm. Within a short time, he worked his way up to a position of large responsibility. In 1858, he married well-to-do Hannah Merritt of South Scituate, who was fourteen years his senior.

A few years after his marriage, he became a partner in a large Boston dry-goods emporium, which became known as Shepherd-Norwell and Company. With his father-in-law's death, the homestead now known as

The partner in this thriving Boston dry-goods emporium gave his name to the town.

the Norwell House became his summer residence and remained so even after the death of Hannah and his subsequent remarriage. When the town embarked upon the task of naming streets in 1870, it seemed appropriate to name the road running by the homestead Norwell Avenue. By this time, Mr. Norwell had become very wealthy in his own right with large property holdings in Florida and also 140 acres of oceanfront adjacent to land owned by Thomas Lawson in the Egypt section of Scituate.

In the 1880s, there was increasing agitation to give the town a greater sense of self-identity by giving South Scituate a new name. One plausible argument given was the prevalence of local mail being delivered to South Scituate, Rhode Island. Also, the town's burgeoning shoe- and box-manufacturing industries would benefit by a completely separate business address from the parent town.

A petition calling for a name change was signed by 278 male residents. (Women at that time were only eligible to vote for school committee members.) Several possible names were being considered when overtures were made to Henry Norwell, suggesting the town might be named for him if he made a large contribution for a new school or for road improvement. Mr. Norwell showed interest in the latter option and pledged a contribution of $2,500 a year for ten years if the town would match his contribution. In the town meeting of March 5, 1888, 255 citizens voted to call the town Norwell with a scattering of votes for other names such as Cushing, Standish and Hatherly.

Mr. Norwell kept his end of the agreement, even though the depression that occurred in the middle 1890s seriously affected his business. He even served as one of the road agents for several years. In February 1903, Henry Norwell died of heart trouble at his winter home in Apoka, Florida. He was survived by his second wife and two children. The Norwell selectmen met to take action on his death. They framed a resolution, part of which, follows: "Although not a native of this town, by his earnest qualities and rare ability, he walked foremost in our ranks…He gave freely for local improvements. He was interested in every movement for the public good. Generous and public spirited, frank and open-hearted, he won a place in our affections rarely to be attained."

Still another noteworthy Norwell philanthropist was summer resident Thomas Gaffield, who also maintained a winter home in Brookline, Massachusetts. One might wonder if his best-known local charitable contribution could have been inspired by the work of another Brookline resident of the time, Frederick Law Olmstead, creator of New York's Central Park and a series of parks around Boston known as the "Emerald Necklace."

Gaffield Park. Children of the twenty-first century still appreciate Mr. Gaffield's gift.

Gaffield, born in Boston in 1825, was educated in the Boston Public Schools and the Lawrence Scientific School. He became a member of a firm specializing in hardware and window glass. In 1863, he began experimenting on the effects of sunlight in changing the color of glass. His work was published in many scientific journals both in this country and abroad. He was also actively engaged in the real estate business in Brookline.

His second wife was Maria Turner of South Scituate, a direct descendant of Humphrey Turner, one of the men of Kent, the original settlers of Scituate. The family spent much time at the Turner homestead, now numbered 761 Main Street. Gaffield was a director of the American Unitarian Association and deeply involved with the YMCA and many other church and benevolent societies relating to destitute children.

In August 1895, the Norwell Selectmen received a letter from Gaffield, who offered them an eight-acre parcel of land lying between River and Forest Streets to be used as a children's park with the stipulation that the town maintain the grounds in perpetuity. The annual 1896 Town Meeting agreed to this condition and set aside Arbor Day, May 1, 1896, for the townspeople to cut trees, clear brush and otherwise prepare the area. There was a great response by the men and boys of the town. The ladies did their part by preparing a wonderful spread served to the volunteers in Fogg Hall.

Although a magnificent gesture on Gaffield's part, it really didn't get the intended use for another century. Norwell historian Joseph Foster Merritt's explanation was that the town was too spread out and that such a park would have worked better in the middle of a city. In recent years, community groups have provided all kinds of playground equipment, and the park is now used by children from all parts of the town.

Upon his death, Mr. Gaffield left books and species of glass and minerals to the Boston Museum of Fine Arts, the Boston Public Library, Massachusetts Institute of Technology and to the James Library. The following is a tribute paid to him in the *Biographical Review of Plymouth County* (1897): "Generations to come will remember this man who, rescued for them, from the grasping hands of modern progress a beauty spot, where childhood and youth may sport in undisturbed innocence and the old dream restfully of the past."

As we recount these examples of local philanthropy, one could speculate whether any of these givers were influenced by the philanthropic philosophy and activity of Andrew Carnegie. Carnegie, a Scottish immigrant like Henry Norwell, amassed a fortune in the steel industry. Late in his life, possibly making amends for his oftentimes-ruthless business practices and exploitation of his workers, Carnegie set an example of philanthropy, which would be emulated by others. In an essay titled "Wealth," he maintained that "a man who dies rich, dies disgraced," and that he would rather leave a son a curse than a million dollars. Carnegie succeeded in giving away $350 million following his selling of Carnegie Steel to J.P. Morgan. He, like Josiah James, made funding libraries a favorite charity, but one that required matching grants from the community.

Self-initiative, thus, was a major ingredient of his philosophy. Owning a magnificent library would not make an educated man if one did not avail himself of its content. The neighboring town of Rockland was one town that accepted a Carnegie grant in 1905, although many of its residents felt that Carnegie's money should be spurned as it was "tainted money."

This survey only "scratches the surface" of Norwell philanthropy, not only in the pecuniary sense, but also in countless instances of people giving of themselves for the betterment of the town. We are now seeing in the first decade of the twenty-first century new kinds of philanthropy in the foundations established by Bill and Melinda Gates and Warren Buffett.

Norwell citizens also continue in works of charity, following the precedents of those who came before them.

CHAPTER 9

WILLIAM GOULD VINAL'S
BOYHOOD DIARY

In the late 1960s, retired professor William Gould Vinal, then well into his eighties, decided the diary he started when he was a young boy, which he continued as a student at Bridgewater Normal School, needed to be updated using 1960s vernacular if later generations were going to understand what a country boyhood was like for a "Back Streeter" (now Grove Street) in turn-of-the century Mount Blue.

Vinal was born in 1881 in a simple late seventeenth-century farmhouse then located at the corner of Grove and Bowker Streets.

It was also the birthplace of Sarah Kent, mother of Dr. L. Vernon Briggs, author of *History of Shipbuilding on the North River*. In 1930, Dr. Briggs presented the house to First Parish Church, along with a sum of money for maintenance. It was moved to a lot adjacent to the church and today is well-known as the Kent House.

In Professor Vinal's diary, he starts out by noting what his teachers at Bridgewater referred to as his chimbley "Chaucer talk" (aint, haint, we-un's) and then highlights contemporary geographical vernacular such as No Pork Hill (Norwell Center), "Bart Barrell" (Lincoln Street), Stockbridge Country (Bound Brook area) and "Snapet" (Assinippi).

Whatever the season, it never occurred to young Willie Gould (or Cap'n Bill, as he became known as later) that he might be bored. In the winter, he and his companions—Eddie Winslow, the Osborne boys, the Richardsons, the Damons and other Mount Blue youth—improvised a double runner, which consisted of two sleds connected by a board. Standing up on this sled and sliding down on Bowker Hill was to experience the "Big Holler." There was no greater thrill than this. At other seasons, the boys would go "skunking," seeking the blacker pelts that would bring two dollars each. Eddie Winslow was the best skinner among them. The going rate for muskrat pelts was ten cents each. He also remembered that every farmer's son saw it as a duty to become adept at killing woodchucks.

Around Decoration Day (Memorial Day), Vinal and George Osborne would go into the woods to get some "crow's foot," a species of moss torn from glacial gravel, often under the shade of a white pine. This brought good money as it was used in wreaths to which flowers were attached for decorating graves on May 30. Summer meant going into the swamps—hopefully some secret spot—and gathering huckleberries, a word used in that era for all kinds of blueberries. High bush berries brought ten cents a quart; low berries, eight cents. The container used was usually a five- or ten-quart lard pail, which was also used for carrying lunch to school. There was great effort to scoop up the berries, both quickly and free of stems and unripe ones. (In my own childhood, I would often hear very frugal people still being described as still having their "blueberry money.")

The genesis of the future naturalist can be seen in his anticipation of seeing the first pussy willow, butterfly, blossoming dandelion and cowslip. A mess of dandelions or cowslip herb was a time-honored spring tonic. May-flowering in Valley Swamp was another annual event. There wasn't the realization then that pulling them up would bring about their extinction. The end of summer meant attending and participating in local country fairs at Marshfield, Weymouth and Brockton. Willie Gould often won ribbons for exhibiting his prize "frizzle" hens.

In the fall of the year, a necessary chore was assisting in "banking" the house, an early form of insulation. A wooden frame about a foot from the foundation was built and filled with pine needles and seaweed. It was also Willie's duty to keep the woodshed filled and to bring in dry wood for the stove.

Willie Gould Vinal attended District Three (corner of Grove and School Streets) for eight years, both summer and winter terms. It was ungraded, with one teacher instructing children from age five to as old as sixteen. Usually, the number of scholars (as pupils were then termed regardless of their level of studiousness) was thirty. The last teacher at District Three, which closed in 1900, was Miss Sarah Bates, who was paid eighty dollars for the winter term of ten weeks. Vinal valued the education he received there, but the facilities and academic offerings were a far cry from that offered in the modern edifice which bears Dr. Vinal's name, which is located just a mile away.

Young Vinal attended high school on the second floor in what is now the Grange Hall on Main Street. In 1896, the high school was moved to the town hall where the Osborn Building (the present town hall) now stands. Although a good student, Vinal mentions several stunts the scholars would play on their teachers. Placing rubber erasers on the wood-burning stoves could mean having to dismiss the school for the remainder of the day. With the relocation of the high school, town meeting appropriated money for a foot bridge that high schoolers used to get from Lincoln Street through the Hoop Pole swamp.

In a small enclave like Mount Blue, folks depended upon one another for company. Card playing (not permitted on Sundays) meant games such as high-low jack, whist and cribbage. Stopping by Henry Ford's store and the Mount

Classmates pose for picture at Mount Blue in 1891. William Gould Vinal, pictured at far right, attended this school for all eight grades.

From the Close of the Civil War to the Turn of the Century

District school no. 3 at
Mount Blue, erected circa
1854.

Blue post office included picking up the mail brought in by Dyer's Express, as well as picking up the local gossip. Vinal remembered how strict Mrs. Ford was—gambling, smoking and drinking by youngsters strictly forbidden. Willie sold newspapers down Stockbridge way, a much busier venue, and also a magazine called the *Lady's Journal*. It was through premiums in selling this magazine that he obtained much of his reading material, such as novels by Robert Louis Stevenson, Fenimore Cooper and Jules Verne.

When it came time for Vinal to go to college, another friend who had planned to go with him had to bow out because his parents decided they couldn't afford to send him. Vinal's parents, on the other hand, said they couldn't afford not to send him. Vinal's future stretched a great distance from Mount Blue. He earned his doctorate degree from Brown University and taught in several colleges, such as Marshall College in West Virginia, Rhode Island College of Education, Western Reserve University and the University of Massachusetts at Amherst. He traveled and lectured all over the world as a renowned naturalist, but the values and experiences of Mount Blue remained with him.

Novelist Thomas Wolfe opined that "you can't go home again." But Willie Gould Vinal did go home again and again. Many of the friends and neighbors of his boyhood remained the friends and neighbors of his old age. He spent many enjoyable and also active years committed to making his boyhood town and neighborhood a better place. He resided in another ancestral home on Grove Street, aptly named "Vinalhaven," until his death in 1973.

CHAPTER 10

OLD TIMES AT MOUNT BLUE

Well into the twentieth century, inhabitants of South Scituate/Norwell were likely to identify with certain village areas within the town. Among them would be Ridge Hill, Accord, Assinippi (Snapet), the Hill (Norwell Center), Church Hill, Sherman's Corner and Mount Blue. Often, the social center of these enclaves was a country store, which also served as the village post office. Here, folks bought groceries, hardware and sundry items needed for everyday living. They also gathered here to "chew the rag" and otherwise ease the often lonely and isolated nature of rural life.

Mount Blue was situated in the northernmost section of the town, almost hemmed in by Hoop Pole Swamp and Burnt Plain Swamp on the south, Valley Swamp on the west and the glacial drumlins of Mount Blue, Mount Hope and Prospect Hill (218 feet above sea level) to the north. Folks here made the best of the glacial soil and swamps that nature afforded them. Many of those living here in former times referred to themselves, often with a good deal of pride, as "Swamp Yankees." They were proud to live in what some perceived to be a less-than-friendly environment, living by the adage "Use up, wear it out, make do, or go without." They bring to my mind a verse from Thomas Gray's "Elegy Written in a Country Churchyard":

> *Let not Ambition mock their useful toil,*
> *Their homely joys and destiny obscure;*
> *Nor Grandeur hear with a disdainful smile*
> *The short and simple annals of the poor.*

A typical Mount Blue home in the early twentieth century.

Henry Ford's Store, earlier Snow Bryant's Tavern, at Bryant's Corner (juncture of Norwell Avenue, Grove and Lincoln Streets), was the Mount Blue post office from the latter part of the nineteenth century down to 1913 when Rural Free Delivery was launched. Another store, just across the way on Lincoln Street, was Isaiah Lincoln's. Ruth Winslow Perry remembers how as a little girl she would get groceries at Lincoln's, paying for them with eggs gathered from her family's chicken coop.

To delineate Mount Blue in today's terms, I would include Mount Blue Street (then called Stockbridge Road), Mount Hope Street, School Street, the eastern end of Grove Street, Norwell Avenue, the northern portion of Bowker Street and Lincoln Street from the Peter Sears homestead (211) northerly toward Mount Blue Street. In earlier times, Mount Blue Street was also referred to as the Mountain Road, which went all the way to Hingham until it was closed off in 1941 when the federal government took land for the naval ammunition depot.

Another notable feature of Mount Blue is Black Pond, known as a "kettle pond," formed about fourteen thousand years ago when the glacier started to melt, and water and sediment collected in a depression. (The drumlin can be approached just behind the Stockbridge Family Cemetery.) Wes Osborne, a longtime Norwell tree warden, explains that the water in

Henry Ford's store and post office, now 3 Norwell Avenue.

Austin Lincoln's store, at the corner of Lincoln and Grove Street, was still operating in the 1930s.

the pond is so acidic that fish cannot live there. Carnivorous plants, such as the Venus fly trap, eat insects for nutrients. Surrounded by twenty-five protected acres, Black Pond became the first nature conservancy site in New England through the efforts of William Gould Vinal. An engraved boulder at the entrance pays homage to Professor Vinal with his symbol sign—a tepee—and the words "A classroom to learn about the unity of life."

THE SOJOURN OF THE ACADIANS

The poet Henry Wadsworth Longfellow chose to write about Evangeline and other French Acadians who were deported from their homeland to Louisiana, but Mount Blue was home to another group of Acadians for a brief time. In 1755, during the Seven Years' War, or the French and Indian War, sixty thousand Acadians were removed, and two thousand of whom were sent to Boston. They were put out to the lowest bidder, who received the results of their labor. Forty were sent to Scituate, and seventeen of these were put in the care of Joseph Clapp, who lived on Cuffee's Lane, a cart path a mile east of Mount Blue. Simon Grandison Cuffee, reputed to be a runaway slave, lived there after his service in the American War for Independence. There are no known descendants left in Norwell of either the Acadians or Cuffee.

Making a Living

Most Mount Blue people "cobbled together" a living on their small farms, but twice each year Mount Blue farmers might have a little extra cash. One of these times was in July and August when the acidic soil of the swamp yielded bountiful crops of blueberries. Also in late November and December, a time known as the "greening time," Mount Bluers would be out in the woods gathering holly, pine and cedar branches, princess pine, winter berries, wild rose hips and seedpods, which they made into wreaths and swags that would be taken into Boston and sold in the Faneuil Hall Marketplace.

In earlier times, commodities such as flour, sugar, molasses and crackers were stored in barrels made from wood from Mount Blue swamps and woodlots. The Hoop Pole Swamp yielded a flexible wood for hoops and cedar and oak for barrel staves to hold dry or wet goods.

Anecdotes from Cap'n Bill

The lifestyle of old Mount Blue has been colorfully chronicled by William Gould Vinal. His column, "Along the North River with Cap'n Bill," often contained reminiscences of the Mount Blue of yesteryear. The following are two excerpts appearing in 1948 that are rich in the local color of his native place:

It was almost proverbial among Mount Blue folk that if a man owned a salt meadow, hauled out plenty of cordwood from his maple swamp, kept a horse and a cow, bought his groceries at Bryant's Corner, and once a year rode to Boston via Dyer's mail coach and the Old Colony, he would surely go to heaven. Just plain ordinary folks with plenty of good common sense and big hearts who live near enough to hear the ocean's roar when there's a northeaster and whose calloused hands were soiled by the dust of the garden and the shoemaker's bench.

I can recall when neighbors were neighbors. The best place to see the old folks really play was at a neighborhood hoedown. They usually occurred in the winter. The parties held at Walt Simmons', Liby Litchfield's and Levi Osborne's stand out in my mind. Willy Stockbridge would bring along his fiddle, and I can see Walt and Liby, well in their eighties, step out pretty lively.

QUINTESSENTIAL SWAMP YANKEES

In my own earlier years, I was personally acquainted with old-timers from Mount Blue who wore their Swamp Yankee heritage as a badge of honor. Even at the present time, the term does not appear in conventional dictionaries, but I recently ran across some descriptive characteristics of these rugged individualists. Here are a few of the best:

Right or wrong he speaks his mind, and he's rarely wrong.
Disagree with him at your own risk.
Believes in hard work and has no use for those who don't.
Doesn't trust the damn fools in Washington or in the state capital either.
As a child, he walked two miles to school every day barefoot, uphill both ways.
And last of all, is honest, self sufficient and will do what he damn well pleases.

I would add another characteristic based upon my own observation. They spoke with carefully chosen words, often laden with sarcasm. Here is a comment from a well-known Mount Blue chauvinist of years gone by (with the usual sting): "Lincoln Street is another highway that keeps its family name. It delves through Bart Barrel's woods to 'Herring Brook Hill' (Norwell Center), reputed to be the place of aristocracy."

To the old-timers and present-day residents alike, Mount Blue has a special unspoiled aspect, a little piece of paradise, *Far From the Madding Crowd*.

From the Close of the Civil War to the Turn of the Century

Above: Mount Bluers Julia Leavitt Osborne (1852–1929) and Levi N. Osborne (1849–1915) are the great-grandparents of the author. Levi was a Civil War veteran in the Sixty-second Regiment, Company A, Massachusetts Infantry.

Right: Mount Bluers Samuel Olson (1865–1931) and Isabel (Osborne) Olson (1880–1966) are the grandparents of the author.

CHAPTER 11

SHOEMAKING IN
SOUTH SCITUATE/NORWELL

At approximately 7 o'clock on the blustery cold evening of March 12, 1901, a raging fire was discovered too late to save the four-story Charles Grose Shoe Factory on High Street from being almost a total loss.

Also devoured by flames was a neighboring residence and stable. The cost of the loss of the buildings and their contents was estimated at $50,000.

Charles Abbott, engineer of the factory, was the first to arrive and managed to crawl into the engine room and tie down the whistle valve that sounded the alarm. Since Norwell had no organized fire department at the time, a bucket brigade was formed by neighbors in an attempt to quell the blaze. The old fire engine, "Constitution," was summoned from South Hingham, but it arrived too late to do any good. The whistle, which sounded until the roof caved in, proved to be the death knell for Grose's and essentially of the major industry of late nineteenth century Norwell.

In that same year, Litchfield's, a thirty-year-old Mansard roof structure located just east of Bryant's Corner on Norwell Avenue, closed with the death of George Litchfield. George was the son of founder John Litchfield and grandfather of Nellie Litchfield Sparrell. These two shops had been the largest employers in Norwell.

William Gould Vinal (Cap'n Bill) reminisced that there had been small shops employing a few craftsmen in virtually every Mount Blue home. He described the shoemaker's bench with "apartments" for pegs and nails and the tools hung behind. The entire shoe was made by these craftsmen who were known as cordwainers. John W. Beal, a well-known local architect,

From the Close of the Civil War to the Turn of the Century

A side yard family shoe shop, which is still standing at 59 High Street.

Litchfield Shoe Factory. Jean and Jim McKenney's residence at 35 Norwell Avenue stands where the factory once was.

recalled how his father, residing on what is now Stetson Shrine Lane, was one of those South Scituate craftsmen who, after completing several pairs of shoes by hand, would walk to Hingham, take the packet to Boston, sell the shoes and return with "findings" for making more shoes.

Vinal points out that these home-based shoemakers found it increasingly hard to compete with the advent of Elias Howe's sewing machine, which was later adapted to sewing leather. Now shoes could be produced one hundred times faster. Claim for this adaptation, which revolutionized the shoe industry, was made by others. An article appeared on January 6, 1905, in the *Rockland Standard*, in which Edwin French of Norwell said it was he, rather than McKay, who devised the shoe-stitching machine. His brother-in-law, Lyman Blake, also took credit. French admitted the idea was Blake's but that he, after months of hard work, came up with a machine that would stitch leather. Both Blake and McKay promised him recompense, but he got nothing. Regardless of who was the rightful inventor, the machine had a phenomenal impact on the shoe industry. The days of the small shop, often referred to as ten footers or twelve footers, were numbered. One of these can still be seen in the side yard at 59 High Street and another on Summer Street, just opposite First Parish Road.

The Charles Grose family of Ridge Hill was among the first local entrepreneurs providing the capital for these new machines housed in factories. Charles, a veteran of the Civil War, was married to Mary Ann Hobart, a member of one of Hingham's oldest families. Their daughter, Mary Frances, married Elwin Temple "E.T." Wright of East Abington, which is now Rockland. For a time, Charles Grose was engaged in the manufacture of shoes with Wright. After this partnership dissolved, Grose purchased the shoe factory of Benjamin Young, currently the Ridge Hill Nursery School. Still later, he acquired a larger building on the west side of High Street. He was assisted in this operation by his son, Charles Webster Grose.

George Christian Turner, who wrote a weekly column in the *Rockland Standard* under the pseudonym the "Circuit Rider," remarked that to get a job in Grose's or Litchfield's was the aspiration of most healthy high school boys resulting in depleted high school classes between 1891 and 1900. Making a weekly wage, if shortsighted, was still more appealing than studying Latin, algebra and ancient history.

In addition to Grose's and Litchfield's, there were several midsized operations such as Charles Young's, Killam and Turner's. During these relatively palmy days for the local shoe industry, Norwell box factories also prospered as the shoes were wholesaled in wooden crates before the advent of corrugated cardboard.

From the Close of the Civil War to the Turn of the Century

A look at the decennial federal census of 1880 reveals that entire South Scituate households—husbands, wives, teenagers and young adult children—were employed in shoemaking. What is also apparent is that the factory system had brought with it a more efficient division of labor. Fifty-eight persons labeled themselves shoe workers, twenty as boot makers, twelve as stitchers, eleven finishers and three shoe cutters. Additionally, seven individuals were listed as shoe manufacturers.

Items in the *Rockland Standard* concerning Grose's and Litchfield's in the 1890s through 1901 reveal that social Darwinism, "survival of the fittest" in the economic realm, was at work as shoemaking became increasingly competitive. Along with the items, I have provided some perspective that the passage of time allows.

On July 14, 1893, stitchers at Charles Grose and Son left work owing to a reduction in prices paid per pair. The firm said they could not pay the former rate because they had begun manufacturing a cheaper grade of shoe. In that same year, a state inspector visited Litchfield's and warned that women and minors must work no more than a fifty-eight-hour week. (As bad as these situations sound, conditions in locally owned industries were generally better than in "bodiless, soulless" corporations since shops like Litchfield's and Grose's employed friends and neighbors and could hardly escape blame if sweatshop conditions existed. It should also be borne in mind that the march toward industrial unionization didn't begin until the 1930s. Also, the first federal ceiling on hours worked and a floor-under-wages legislation were not enacted until also the 1930s.)

A January 5, 1894 article reported that Grose's was resuming operations after several weeks' layoff. This was during the time of the severe banking panic and depression that had begun in 1893. Although there had been depressions in the 1830s, the 1850s and the 1870s, the one beginning in 1893 was much more severe as it was the first depression to hit an increasingly industrialized and urban society. Manufacturing in Norwell, however, had remained secondary to largely subsistence-type agriculture. (Norwell folks still had their wood lots, vegetable gardens, small barnyards, and hunting and fishing prowess to fall back upon.)

On April 15, 1894, an article reported that the Grose shop was about to go out of business. (Apparently business picked up. A subsequent article, on November 25, 1895, reported that work was about to begin on remodeling, and that it was expected that the factory would be in operation again before the first of January.)

Individual proprietorship with its inherent risks changed at Grose's with its incorporation at Portland, Maine, on December 16, 1898. Ridge Hill Boot and Shoe Company, with a capital stock of $150,000, was incorporated. Charles W. Grose was elected secretary, and treasurer and Charles Lapham was named superintendent. A fifty-horse-power boiler was installed, and so things stood until the disastrous fire.

Fortunately, the shoe factories in Rockland and Brockton remained viable, and the "electrics" were operating regular runs to the "shoe town" (Rockland) and the "shoe city" (Brockton). E.T. Wright's in Rockland was to become even more prosperous with the "Wright arch preserver" built into quality shoes.

William Gould Vinal provides us with a charming scene full of imagery with his description of "Shoe Makers' Trail." "Every morning, shoe workers heading for the Assinippi trolley would cross lots from Lincoln Street and Grove Street with lighted kerosene lanterns leaving them at Henry Main's on Prospect Street and picking them up upon their return to light their way home."

For good or bad, Norwell never did become an important shoe center like many of the surrounding towns. If there was a single overriding reason for this, it would have to be the isolation of Norwell and the consequent difficulty in acquiring raw materials and marketing the finished product. Despite much agitation to do so, the town never allowed the Old Colony Railroad to lay tracks through Norwell linking the Hanover Branch with Greenbush. Norwell, thus, remained a "backwater" as far as industrial development was concerned until the completion of the new Route 3 in the early 1960s.

CHAPTER 12

TO THE FARMHOUSE BORN,
TO THE MANOR HOUSE WED

How dear to this heart are the scenes of my childhood when fond recollection present them to view." These are the opening lines of Samuel Woodworth's poem immortalizing scenes that present themselves just over the Norwell line in Greenbush. Woodworth's verses might just as well apply to the historic Jacobs farmhouse and barn and adjacent outbuildings and extensive fields that Norwell historian Joseph Foster Merritt thusly described as "an unspoiled gem of rural charm and scenic loveliness."

The Jacobs homestead dates back to 1726 with a later 1839 addition to the east, called "the other house." The last Jacobs family members to reside in the house were Mr. and Mrs. Barton Jacobs and their two sons, Henry Barton and Frederick Boynton. By 1939, the farmhouse and surrounding acreage was placed in the care of the New England Society for the Preservation of Antiquities, now officially called "Historic New England."

Henry Barton and Frederick Boynton showed remarkable promise from their earliest years. The former went on to become an eminent physician and cosmopolite while the latter's life ended at the age of thirty-one. Even in the latter part of the nineteenth century, consumption, also known as tuberculosis, was still taking many in the prime of life. While Frederick was destined to lie prematurely in the Union Cemetery in Assinippi, Henry Barton scaled the heights, both professionally and socially. Henry Barton prepared at Hingham High School for Philips Exeter and Harvard College. After graduation from Harvard Medical School, he engaged in research at Johns Hopkins in Baltimore and became an authority on the treatment of tuberculosis.

Frederick prepared at Rockland High School for Philips Exeter and Harvard. Following graduation from Harvard Law, he was admitted to the Suffolk County Bar Association. At the same time, he remained devoted to his native town, becoming a major advocate for both a street railway and, as a school committee member, for obtaining a regional superintendent of schools. Both objectives came to fruition. Increasingly failing health aborted Frederick's career. Dr. Henry Barton exhibited much generosity in a vain attempt to restore his brother to health. In 1893, he sent the family $500 so father, mother and brother could attend the Chicago World's Fair. His brother made it possible for Frederick to seek cures in sanitariums in Atlanta; Asheville, North Carolina; and Saranac Lake. From Saranac Lake, Frederick returned to his home in Assinippi where he died on September 2, 1896.

After his brother's death, young Dr. Jacobs continued the role of dutiful son to the now widowed "Mrs. Barton," the name by which she was usually referred. As regularly as the first robins appeared in the spring time and a flock of geese being sighted flying south in the autumn, the *Rockland Standard* would report Dr. Jacobs's arrival in Assinippi to accompany his mother to Baltimore, where she would spend the winter, and again in April, returning with her to Assinippi. In the spring, he would remain for several days pruning trees, repairing stone walls and otherwise pursuing the same farm chores he had as a youth.

From 1888 to 1896, he served as personal physician to Robert Garrett, president of the Baltimore and Ohio Railroad. Mrs. Garrett was a member of the Henry Clay Frick family. Frick had been a business partner of steel tycoon Andrew Carnegie and later became his bitter adversary. Garrett had become mentally ill, believing he was the Prince of Wales, later King Edward VII (1901–1910). Garrett was served by a full complement of servants, and the household was run as if it were Buckingham Palace, maintaining his grand delusion. After Mr. Garrett's death, Dr. Jacobs returned to his work at Johns Hopkins.

On November 7, 1902, an item in the *Rockland Standard* reported that Dr. and Mrs. Henry Barton Jacobs of Baltimore had spent a portion of the previous week at Dr. Jacobs's former home. Dr. and Mrs. Jacobs had been married the previous spring and had just returned from a European wedding trip. Mrs. Jacobs was the widow of Robert Garrett, formerly president of the Baltimore and Ohio Railroad. The news item went on to report the marriage had caused quite a sensation in Baltimore. One can assume it had no less an effect in Assinippi. The remainder of Dr. Jacobs's life was spend in the nouveaux riches pattern of winters in Baltimore, spring and early summer in Europe, and the summer "season" at Whiteholme in Newport. The *Standard* of July 22, 1904, reported on the exclusive Newport circle known as the "Two Hundred," of which Dr. and Mrs. Jacobs were listed as members. The derivation of this term comes from the number of persons, the "Four Hundred," that could be accommodated in Mrs. Astor's Fifth Avenue ballroom for her receptions and soirees. The article did not mention whether the Jacobses were invited to Mrs. Astor's as were members of the "cream of New York society."

Norwell historian Ann Henderson has recorded Dr. Jacobs's apparent disenchantment with trailing his wife each spring through the salons of Paris as she sought the latest fashions. He wrote his mother, saying: "In spite of all the beauties of the old and new worlds, your quiet life in that peaceful little spot is more happy and more to be desired than all the lives of the kings and queens of France."

"Mrs. Barton" died in 1921 followed by her companion, who had been kept on full salary, five years later. For many years, the farm had been managed by Mr. George Turner, Mrs. Jacobs's cousin. Mr. Turner, his wife, Mertie, and their three children lived in the eastern wing.

Mrs. Henry Barton Jacobs died in 1931, followed by her husband eight years later. Dr. Jacobs, a longtime vice president of the Society for the Preservation of New England Antiquities (SPNEA), bequeathed to them care of the property, which consisted of the farmhouse, barn, stables, etcetera, on thirty-three acres on both sides of Main Street and northward on Jacobs Lane. He included in his bequest $22,000 for maintenance.

Unfortunately, the two mills, created from the damming of the Third Herring Brook, no longer existed. The gristmill had disappeared at some uncertain date and the saw mill had succumbed to fire as the result of a Fourth of July prank in 1920.

In 1989, the SPNEA (today known as "Historic New England") allowed the town of Norwell to purchase the property, although there were covenants allowing the society to maintain preservation rights to protect the buildings and open spaces that distinguished the property. Care of the east wing, the "other house," was taken on by the Norwell Historical Society with the oversight of the Norwell Historical Commission. This section is open on request for private showings and, for the past several years in June, has been the site of the Strawberry Festival and the historical society's Christmas Open House.

Oil by unknown artist of Jacobs grist and saw mills, circa 1830.

The Jacobs homestead. Notice the distinct rooflines that delineate the two houses.

Dr. Henry Barton Jacobs, noted tuberculosis specialist at Johns Hopkins.

From the Close of the Civil War to the Turn of the Century

Right: Dr. Henry Barton Jacobs
and Mary Frick Garrett Jacobs of
Baltimore and Newport.

Below: Whiteholme, the Jacobs's
"cottage" at Newport.

CHAPTER 13

NORWELL SAYS "YES" TO THE TROLLEY BUT "NO" TO THE TRAIN

.

Clang, clang, clang went the trolley;
Ding, ding, ding went the bell;
Zing, zing, zing went my heartstrings as we started for the Huntington Dell.
—*Judy Garland in* Meet Me in St. Louis, *1944*

Possibly nothing opened up Norwell more to additional social, educational and employment opportunities at the turn of the century than did the trolley.

But despite "mixed signals" from time to time, the prospect of a train passing through the town never materialized. The Hanover Branch of the Old Colony division of the New York, New Haven and Hartford Railroad remained a branch.

June 22, 1896, was a gala day in Norwell with the opening of the Hanover Street Railway. Flags and bunting decorated the four open and two closed cars, each of which contained ten reversible seats. The line connected with the Rockland and Abington Company at Union Street in Rockland. The original intent was for the line to operate east on Webster Street—Route 123—to Assinippi Corner. The directors, however, petitioned the Norwell and Hanover Selectmen to allow them to build from Mann's Corner in North Hanover and then proceed north on Main Street in Hanover and down High Street in Norwell, to Washington Street to Queen Anne's Corner, where it would connect with the Hingham line. Thus, the Hanover Street Railway would operate over a six-mile route.

From the Close of the Civil War to the Turn of the Century

The line was capitalized at $10,000 with shares selling at $100 each. There were two turnabouts built, one on Webster Street near Mann's Corner and the other just beyond Assinippi Corner near the Norwell line. A car barn with a capacity for eight cars, a superintendent's office and an employee's room would be built opposite the Grove on High Street.

The construction took only two months from start to finish, with Italian immigrant workers employed to lay the tracks, each of which was ten feet long and weighed over a thousand pounds each. Electricity for the overhead wires was purchased from an Abington power company.

Later, plans were formulated to extend the line down Main Street through Norwell Center and on to Scituate Harbor and Cohasset. It was thought that Norwell, with its cheap land and stately homes, might become a streetcar suburb such as those growing up around Boston and other cities. But a combination of factors such as neighborhood opposition and management concerns as to whether the extension would pay thwarted the project. For many of the same reasons, the section of Washington Street from Oak Street to Assinippi Corner was never built. An early schedule for the line, later absorbed by the Bay State Company, called for the first car to leave Queen Anne's Corner for Rockland at 5:30 a.m. and from Assinippi at 6:35 p.m. The last car from Rockland would leave at 10:00 p.m. Fare for the whole route cost $0.05, with another $0.10 allowing one to ride on the Hingham line to Nantasket.

On Labor Day weekend in 1897, the *Rockland Standard* reported that the cars were always full leaving for Nantasket every fifteen minutes. The *Standard* also reported that in one summertime week, Ridge Hill Grove was the site for outings for the Union Glee Club of Rockland, the Ancient Order of Hibernians of Abington, the Odd Fellows, the South Hingham firemen and a baseball game between the Emerson Shoe Factory of Rockland and Winthrop's of Abington. The electrics allowed everyone to be on the move.

But the heyday of the electrics locally was brief with the greater use of automobiles and jitney buses for short trips. Gradually, schedules were pared down, and in 1917, the Bay State Company voted to discontinue the portion of the line from Mann's Corner to Assinippi. There was an outcry of protest both from local riders and the businessmen of Rockland. Representatives from both groups brought their protests before the Public Services Commission. The line was granted a "stay," but the inevitable end came on December 9, 1920.

The Hanover Branch Remains a Branch

Early in the second decade of the twentieth century, it appeared highly probable that Norwell would get train service. Ostensibly at any rate, it appeared that most of Norwell's business and civic leaders were in favor. A May 12, 1912 article in the *Rockland Standard* told of a meeting having been held regarding extending the Hanover Branch from Hanover Four Corners across country to Greenbush, which would put Rockland on the main line. Present at the Boston meeting, which was held in the office of Timothy Byrnes, vice president of the New York, New Haven and Hartford Railroad, were Horace Fogg and Ernest Sparrell, who both represented a committee appointed by Norwell at a recent town meeting. Editorially, the *Standard* opined that the people of Norwell wanted such a line and would do almost anything to get it.

Later in the year, when the proposed route was outlined, it was obvious that trouble was brewing. The route would cut through the estate of the wealthy Sylvester family and also the poultry farms of Henry Tolman and Henry Smith, cutting them in two. Riverdale Farm, owned by Henry A. Turner and sons, would be divided, with the track coming between the house and the barn. Professor Solon Bailey and his brother Dr. M.H. Bailey, both of Harvard, had two summer places on the bank of the North River. The proposed railroad would come between the two houses.

Almost a year later, on April 25, 1913, the *Standard* reported that Horace Fogg had received a letter from railroad president Mellen, saying, "The present business outlook is such [there was a countrywide recession occurring at the time] that we do not feel we can justify, the expenditure of capital."

Thus, Norwell remained an economic "backwater" through two world wars and a major depression in the eyes of many observers. With improved roads, trucks began carrying more and more freight, and most residents felt that the bucolic solitude that remained in Norwell was an adequate payoff for not having a railroad.

Helen Fogg, daughter of Horace Fogg, put the onus of not having a railroad squarely on the shoulders of her influential father. Horace, a graduate of Harvard and scion of one of Norwell's most prestigious families, followed both his grandfather and father as treasurer of the South Scituate Savings Bank. He also served as town treasurer and treasurer of Plymouth County. In 1907, he was one of the founders of the Rockland Trust Company and later became its president. In 1930, as president of the Marshfield Horticultural and Agricultural Society, he was on the bandstand introducing the lieutenant governor of Massachusetts when he collapsed and died. Over the years, he was responsible for bringing many notable political figures, such as Henry Cabot Lodge Sr., to Norwell on various ceremonial occasions.

Norwell's Ruth Chipman Bailey, in her biography of Helen Fogg, Where in the World?, quoted Helen concerning Norwell's projected railroad. It is obvious from her remarks that she felt strongly, not necessarily approvingly, that her father played a commanding role in keeping the railroad at bay: "My father knew about the progress of mankind—but the railroad did not figure into his scheme of advance. He threw his energy and influence into blocking the cockeyed plan which would have run tracks through lovely stretches of woodland with danger from flying sparks, and would have brought little factories making tacks or shoes in its wake. But most of all, it would have brought outsiders, foreigners, into our midst and with them would certainly come the devil and booze and heaven knew what other nameless evils."

Norwell streetcars come and go near intersection of High and Washington Streets.

"The Hill" in the 1930s.

Faculty of Norwell High School in 1938 as shown in the yearbook the *Shipbuilder*.

PART 3

The Early Twentieth Century in Norwell

CHAPTER 14

THE MOTORCAR AGE
COMES TO NORWELL

In the early 1900s, the sighting of an automobile on Main Street or Washington Street in Norwell was an event that made the newspapers.

Automobile ownership remained a rarity in our community, as well as in others, until well into the second decade of the new century. The horse still reigned supreme. Although some were raising thoroughbreds, like Arthur Power at May Elmsand by Henry Norwell at his estate, most of our citizens owned workhorses that were used mainly for farm labor and work on the roads. On special occasions, "Old Dobbin" would be hitched to a wagon for local jaunts. According to the federal census of 1900, there were only eight thousand automobiles in the United States and eighteen million horses and mules.

An individual highly respected in the village was still the blacksmith, such as Civil War veteran Frank Alger who operated a smithy at Assinippi Corner. It was recorded in the *Rockland Standard* of January 18, 1901, that he had shod twenty-two horses in a day and ninety-one in a week. The prevalent cold weather meant that smooth horseshoes had to be replaced to allow the horse to get a grip on the icy surfaces.

Early automobiles such as the Stanley Steamer and the Baker Electric were totally impractical for all but the shortest trips. The future American president Woodrow Wilson, the president of Princeton University, saw them as toys that displayed the "arrogance of the rich." Even with Henry Ford's gasoline-powered engine, the horseless carriage remained out of the reach of most.

The Early Twentieth Century in Norwell

But increasingly, the *Standard* would report on some of Norwell's more economically favored acquiring machines with now familiar names like Oldsmobile, Packard and Studebaker, along with less-familiar names as Reo, Peerless, Columbia, and the Cole. Reverend Charles Howard Gale of our Unitarian Church, like comedian Jack Benny, became the owner of a Maxwell touring car.

The *Standard* issue of January 8, 1909, announced that Frank Staples had visited the town in his new automobile during the previous week and called on several friends. A *Standard* story of the same time carried a tone of sarcasm describing an auto being towed by a horse with the barb: "it looks as if the good horse is here to stay." But Dr. Little was betting on the auto prevailing by building an "automobile house" at his home on Main Street.

The year was 1908 when Henry Ford introduced his Model T, the "Tin Lizzie," at a price of $850. Eventually the price went down to $360, with black being the only color available. By 1914, Ford was paying his assembly line workers the then unheard-of sum of $40 a week. Now Ford workers could also become Ford customers.

Most of the cars of this era were roofless touring cars. Before the self-starter was introduced, the crank was reaping a harvest of broken arms and scarred chins. Gradually, driving became less hazardous with carbide headlights and improved braking and steering mechanisms.

Drivers were being warned in the *Standard* to beware of "auto traps" set up on the road to Rockland. Those traveling at speeds of twenty miles per hour were subject to arrest and fines.

One of the first Tarvia roads in town came in 1915 when town meeting appropriated $2,500 to put down a macadam surface on Main Street from Norwell Center to Assinippi Corner. The State Highway Commission was to put up a matching sum with the roadwork being done under the supervision of the Massachusetts Highway Commission.

Possibly the most tragic local automobile accident of the time occurred on May 30, 1913. One of Norwell's best-known couples, Mr. and Mrs. Ebenezer Fogg, were killed when a train struck their automobile while they were crossing near the Kenberma Station at Nantasket. Mrs. Fogg was decapitated and Mr. Fogg died shortly after being admitted to the hospital. Their son, Harry T. Fogg, treasurer of the South Scituate Savings Bank, brought suit against the New York, New Haven, and Hartford Railroad, asking for $25,000 in damages for the loss of each parent. A settlement was reached with $6,951 for Ebenezer and $6,503 for his mother. The introduction of traffic lights, first in New York City in 1922, would reduce the number of such tragedies.

Throughout the teen years of the new century, there were frequent announcements appearing of jitney buses and closed taxis being put into use. These vehicles provided more flexibility for short trips than streetcars could give. With more cars and trucks on the road, the trolley lines were reducing their schedules.

The following are a few such notices, which appeared in the *Rockland Standard*:

> *September 15, 1915—the jitney bus will leave Rockland at 1:15 p.m., fifteen minutes later to accommodate students from Norwell attending Rockland High School.*
>
> *February 12, 1917—John Sparrell of Sparrell's Garage* [located where the Quik Pik is now] *recently put into use a closed car for his Greenbush taxi service.*
>
> *February 6, 1918—On Friday, four large cars took passengers from Norwell to Rockland for shopping.*

Perhaps the last time "Get a Horse" was heard in Norwell was during the bitterly cold winter of 1920. Sparell's taxi, carrying mail and passengers to Greenbush, was stalled in the snow and had to be hauled out by a horse.

Two ads on the same newspaper page. The horse did not surrender easily to the horseless carriage!

The Early Twentieth Century in Norwell

The 1920s began with a triumph for the automobile when, on March 4, 1921, Warren G. Harding became the first president to ride to his inauguration in an automobile, a Packard Twin Six. The twenties was a prosperous decade for many, with automobile production and associated industries leading the way. Road and bridge construction, gasoline stations, overnight cabins and roadside eateries created jobs for millions. Henry Ford, responsible more than any other man for putting Americans on wheels, introduced his first new model in eighteen years, the Model A, in 1927. In order to compete with rival automobile companies, he also now gave his customers a choice of color.

The Norwell town report of 1929 was the first to list the number of autos in the town of 1,519 residents. There were 758 autos and only ninety-six horses. This number translates to there being pretty close to one automobile for every two inhabitants. The automobile would eventually contribute to Norwell's phenomenal growth in ways unimagined in 1929.

CHAPTER 15

CHALLENGES OF A
RURAL SCHOOL SYSTEM IN THE
EARLY TWENTIETH CENTURY

By the first decade of the twentieth century, the small town of Norwell had partially abandoned a remaining vestige of colonial public education, the district school. The community's motivation was both financial and pedagogical.

Letting go of the ancient system would not only mean fewer schools to staff, heat and keep in repair, but it would also result in a more equitable educational opportunity for all the children. Some schools, such as District Three at Mount Blue, had one teacher responsible for all eight grades. Now, with the closing of District Three and also District Two, presently Grange Hall, each teacher in the remaining districts would be responsible for only two or three grades. This change also meant that, for the first time, the town was responsible for transporting scholars outside their district. The town appropriated three hundred dollars for Ben Loring to transport children from Mount Blue to Norwell Center in the "school barge." But despite the positive good brought about by consolidation, there still remained challenges peculiar to a country school system such as Norwell's.

The earlier joint prudential and school committee arrangement for operating the schools had been abolished in 1866. The former group had been responsible for hiring teachers and maintaining school buildings in its respective districts. What remained was a three-member school committee overseeing the education of the entire town. During this period and down to the present time, there was usually at least one woman on the board since the Massachusetts legislature had granted the distaff side the right to vote for school committee and also the right to sit on the panel. Longtime District Five teacher Marian Merritt served for a few years in the 1890s until a state judicial ruling disallowed a locally employed teacher to concurrently serve on that town's committee. However, Nellie L. Sparrell, who was a former Norwell teacher, served continuously from 1917 to 1962.

In 1893, a union superintendency composed of Norwell, Hanover and Hanson had been formed, and it lasted for more than sixty years. Throughout this period, there was recurring interest in the possible advantages of having a regional high school. The first union superintendent was Mr. A.J. Curtis. The three towns paid half of his salary with the state picking up the rest.

The establishment of a public high school, a bone of contention in town since 1870, finally materialized in 1888, with the first class graduating in 1891. Norwell's first high school occupied the second story of what is now the Grange Hall at the corner of Main and South Streets. In 1896, the high school was moved to the town hall building located approximately on the site of the present town hall.

In 1900, there were 167 scholars enrolled in grades one through twelve. In that year, the total school budget amounted to $3,600. Compare that to the 2007 budget, which was in excess of $16 million dollars with a per pupil cost exceeding $9,000. Teachers then were paid $190 for the three-month winter term and $250 for the spring and summer term. By 1910, salaries ranged from $10.50 to $12 per week, and there were 266 scholars enrolled.

For the lower grades, local young women who had graduated from Bridgewater Normal or the Quincy Training School usually worked out best because they knew country conditions and did not have to pay room and board, as they usually lived at home with their parents. But school committee and superintendent reports of the time echoed the concern that after one or two years' experience, higher-paying neighboring towns recruited them.

The tenure of superintendents and high school principals early in the twentieth century tended to be relatively brief. Superintendents following Mr. Curtis were James Hayes, Charles Harris, and Stephen Bean. Among those following the first high school headmaster, Edward Cox, were F.W. Carrier, John C. Page, and J.M. Nichols.

Norwell's high school had both a good and bad year in 1909. The seniors held a successful fair the previous fall, with chances sold to win a live pig, a rooster and two hens. The proceeds helped finance a senior trip to Washington, D.C., the highlight of which was a private meeting with President Taft. A less positive occurrence was a fracas that took place at the high school. On May 14, 1909, Principal Bemis grabbed a lad by the shoulder for lying on his desk during school hours. A general mêlée followed, which was broken up by Assistant Principal W. Scott Osborne. Several girls became hysterical, and school had to be dismissed for the day. As a result of the incident, Principal Bemis was notified of his dismissal. Bemis vowed he would not go without a hearing. The subsequent hearing upheld his dismissal.

A small high school of between fifty and sixty was difficult to operate with only a teaching principal and one or two assistants. They were expected to follow a highly academic curriculum mandated by the state. The high school law of 1898 required them to prepare pupils for state normal schools, colleges and scientific institutions, as well as for purposes of general culture. With the limited staff, Latin and other foreign languages, as well as higher math, physics and chemistry, could be offered only in alternate years. The 1908 town report contained a statement from Principal Carrier that in the context of present-day values would be considered anti-intellectual. He maintained that the high school should prepare students for life here in Norwell. He would accept history, science, mathematics and modern foreign languages being offered, but felt Latin should be banished from the curriculum.

It wasn't until 1918 that Norwell diverted from a general curriculum for all by offering a business course. Two typewriters were purchased and a teacher of commercial subjects was hired.

Graduating classes in the first two decades of the century invariably numbered less than ten, with the number of girls exceeding boys. Boys were prone to withdraw from school after the eighth grade to work on farms or gain employment in shoe factories in neighboring towns. For example, the Class of 1909 had seven girls and one boy. The graduating Class of 1913 consisted of seven girls and no boys. Also in 1913, there was a new state child labor law that mandated children remain in school long enough to demonstrate ability to read, write and spell equal to a fourth-grade level.

In 1914, with only four seniors, the school committee allowed members of the junior class to graduate a year early. A member of the Class of 1914 was perhaps one of the most distinguished alumnus of Norwell High up to that time. Louis Lyons went on to graduate from Massachusetts Agricultural College. Following service in the World War, Lyons went to work for the *Boston Globe* as a reporter. Soon he was writing editorials that were syndicated nationally. His work as a war correspondent during World War II earned him the honor of being one of the first recipients of a Neiman Fellowship at Harvard. Between 1946 and 1964, he held the post of curator of the Neiman Awards. In 1921, Lyons married Margaret Tolman of Church Hill.

The Early Twentieth Century in Norwell

Two other graduates of this time were beloved teachers and principals who had schools named in their honor. They were Ella Osborne Osborn, Class of 1911, and Grace Farrar Cole, Class of 1917.

Regular trolley runs between Rockland and Norwell made it possible for several young people from Norwell to attend the much-larger Rockland High School. For instance, in 1918, there were five students from Norwell who graduated from Rockland. Among them were Margaret Crowell Dumas, an indefatigable community activist who served as town treasurer from 1943 to 1961.

Elementary education was enriched in 1900 with the hiring of A. Gertrude Jones as a drawing teacher and with the introduction of a formal program of music education in 1912. But the strongest plea from the school committee and professional educators was the need of further consolidation of the elementary schools. This was finally achieved in 1922 when the town appropriated $40,000 to construct a new high school to be attached to the town hall. High-school classes were held on the second floor, while grades five through eight occupied the first. Primary classes were held in the three remaining district schools.

Throughout the period, matters of attendance and school hygiene were constantly addressed. Parents were taken to task for not insisting their children attend school regularly. A particularly bad time for attendance was during the "greening time" in December. Many young people preferred to make money gathering greens for sale in the Boston market rather than attending school. To encourage good attendance, names of pupils with perfect attendance were published in the town report and in the newspaper.

But the poor attendance was often the result of sickness exacerbated by crowded classrooms, which were stifling hot at the front near the stove and freezing in the rear. On February 1, 1907, 50 percent of the scholars were absent because of scarlet fever, measles or whooping cough. In October 1915, all the schools were closed because of an epidemic of measles. All schools were again closed during the influenza epidemic of 1918.

The following excerpt from Stephen Bean's 1918 report places in perspective how our school system managed to evolve with another concern unique in rural schools, the outhouse problem.

The nuisances attendant of most rural schools is a perennial problem. Of course, flush closets are not to be expected in places where running water is not available, but there are on the market so many devices designed to ameliorate this undesirable condition and at no great expense. It seems a pity to find the old type of sanitary facilities in use in any town in this progressive state.

Indoor toilets or not, one may evince from the preceding paragraphs that much upgrading in our local schools had occurred by the 1920s. Further improvements were to come despite the Great Depression and another world war. Beginning in the 1950s with a changing population pattern and new concerns, such as the Soviet triumph in space with the 1957 launching of Sputnik, quantum leaps came in the following decades, continuing down to the present with Norwell now being able to boast of having one of the premier school systems in the entire state.

Students of Norwell Center School, circa 1914.

The Early Twentieth Century in Norwell

At school in Norwell in the early 1900s.

Staff and students of Norwell High School in 1918.

Left: Three of the Norwell High School graduates in 1917: Fred Frederickson (from left), Russell Olson and Otto Olson.

Below: A program of graduation exercises on June 14, 1917. Note the war-related student speeches.

NORWELL HIGH SCHOOL

GRADUATION EXERCISES

THURSDAY EVENING, JUNE 14, 1917

SEVEN FORTY-FIVE O'CLOCK

...PROGRAMME...

"ITALIA" (Donizetti)   John Gutterson

PRAYER,   The Reverend Howard Charles Gale

SALUTATORY,
          Grace E. Farrar

"The Terror of the Sea."
          Fred C. Joseph

School Chorus, "Faith to Win."   (Bullard)

"The Red Cross Nurse at The Front."
          Ruth E. Kidder

"Back to the Farm."
          F. Russell Olson

"TRAUMEREI" (Schumann)   John Gutterson

CLASS HISTORY,
          Minnie F. Gardner

CLASS PROPHECY,
          Charles W. Leggett

School Chorus, "Glad Festal Day,"   (Bizet)

"The Children's Crusade" with VALEDICTORY.
          Miriam F. Ford

Presentation of Gift.

Presentation of Diplomas.

Benediction.

Director of Music   Rosalie H. Wheelock
     Organist   John Gutterson
     Accompanist   Marian Boynton, '19

CHAPTER 16

ARSENIC AND OLD ASSINIPPI

In 1877, the South Scituate correspondent for the *Rockland Standard* newspaper bemoaned the scarcity of news from the community: "A revival of the high school interest [whether or not the town should support a public high school] or even a mad dog incident would be refreshing."

Truthfully, most of the news emanating from the town in addition to the mundane notes of births, marriages and deaths were accounts of whist parties and church socials. But all of that changed early in the next century with Norwell making the headlines.

It might be noted here that headlines were a comparatively new device first popularized by competing journalists Hearst and Pulitzer in the sensational "yellow" journalism of the time. Norwell was the scene of a mysterious death and subsequent murder trial in Plymouth that caught the attention of the whole nation.

In 1907, Admiral Joseph Giles Eaton had decided to spend his retirement years in Assinippi after completing a successful naval career. Eaton and his much-younger second wife, Jennie May Harrison Eaton, purchased the Dr. Franklin Jacobs estate on Washington Street. Today, looking much as it did a century ago, the Eatons' former residence is an office building now numbered 427 Washington Street. The Eaton family circle also included Mrs. Eaton's mother and two daughters from Mrs. Eaton's previous marriage, June and Dorothy Ainsworth. The entire family was well liked and quickly entered into the social life of the village.

Born in Alabama in 1847, Eaton graduated from Annapolis in 1867 ranking sixth in his class. His distinguished naval career was highlighted by his service in the Spanish-American War of 1898 and the Filipino Insurrection in 1900. Among the famous ships he had commanded were the USS *Massachusetts* and the USS *Oregon*.

A baby boy was "apparently" born to the Eatons in March 1909. Although there was an announcement of the birth in the *Rockland Standard*, it was never recorded by the Norwell town clerk. Despite the happy event, rumors abounded that the marriage was not a happy one, and that the child had actually been adopted. Tragically, the five-month-old baby died suddenly in August at the Eaton summer cottage in Scituate. Mrs. Eaton demanded that an autopsy be performed, which revealed the infant had died of natural causes. At the burial in Union Cemetery in Assinippi a few days later, only Admiral Eaton and the sexton of the Unitarian Church were present, with Admiral Eaton reading the committal prayers.

On March 14, 1913, a stunning headline reported the sudden death of Admiral Eaton of Assinippi. An autopsy raised questions as to the cause of the death, and the viscera were sent to Professor Whitney of Harvard Medical School for examination. The widow and her entire household were placed under surveillance. A funeral for Admiral Eaton was held at the residence with the Reverend Houghton of the Unitarian Church officiating.

An inquest was held in Hingham Court, resulting in Mrs. Eaton's arrest on the charge of murder in the first degree for having given arsenic to her husband. She was held without bail in Plymouth Jail. Later, Mrs. Eaton was indicted by the Plymouth County grand jury. The April 8, 1913 issue of the *Standard* reported that it was rumored there would be a second inquest, and that a second arrest was imminent. The *Standard* also reported on the excitement that pervaded over the once-quiet neighborhood: "Every stranger who arrived on the car (streetcar) in Assinippi is looked upon as one of those 'writer boys' as reporters became known in town."

The Eaton trial began in Plymouth County Superior Court on October 13, 1913. One of the sites visited by the jurors was the Eaton home in Assinippi. Among the local witnesses called were medical examiner Gilman Osgood and undertaker Lyman Wadsworth. It soon became apparent that the prosecution possessed only circumstantial evidence; no one had actually seen Mrs. Eaton administer arsenic to her husband. The government set out to prove that jealousy was the motive and that Mrs. Eaton had a wealthy suitor in the West and wanted her husband out of the way. Miss Dorothy Ainsworth testified for the defense that she believed that Admiral Eaton had actually poisoned the baby who had died in Scituate in 1909. Mrs. Eaton was reported as holding up well, maintaining her composure at all times.

After a trial lasting more than two weeks, Mrs. Eaton was acquitted by the jury that had remained "out" for more than nine hours. Mrs. Eaton was then immediately released and returned to her home, receiving a cordial welcome by many of her neighbors. She was also the recipient of many congratulatory telegrams from all over the country. When asked about future plans, the widow would only say she was glad to be home. On December 12, 1913, an item in the *Standard* reported that Governor Foss had notified Mrs. Eaton that he could not grant her request to help her obtain reimbursement from the state for expenses in defending herself.

One last local news entry on that dysfunctional family appeared February 1, 1917, with the bizarre news that Mrs. Eaton's daughter, Mrs. June Ainsworth Keyes, had been removed to the Taunton Hospital for the Insane at the request of her mother, Mrs. Jennie Eaton Ainsworth. (Mrs. Eaton had apparently reverted to using the name of her first husband.)

By this date, the residents of the town were probably more interested in the fact that Union Bridge had collapsed and that President Wilson's valiant attempts to maintain American neutrality in the world war were breaking down with the imperial German government's announcement of the resumption of unrestricted U-boat warfare. By the end of the century, those residents who personally remembered the circumstances and dramatis personae of the Eaton affair were no longer living. The case remained unsolved.

The Admiral Eaton place in Assinippi.

CHAPTER 17

THEY WERE GOOD YEARS
AND GOOD TIMES

The decade and a half prior to the First World War (1914–1918) is often referred to as the "Good Years," taken from the title of a social history relating to the era written by Walter Lord, who was also the author of *A Night to Remember*, about the sinking of the Titanic in 1912.

Relative to the years preceding and following, these years were good times to be alive in America and to live in a rural community such as Norwell. True, citizens were earning less than stellar wages, but they were still able to enjoy a myriad of social diversions within the town at very little cost.

Nationally, too, real wages were still low and hours long, but there was a spirit of reform abroad in the land, which was resulting in a better quality of life for most. Theodore Roosevelt, known as Teddy or TR, was president (1901–1909), with an optimism and joie de vivre that was infectious. As one contemporary recalled, "There was such fun in the man. I am so glad I was alive when he was president." But few Americans could imagine that a great world conflict was looming, and even fewer could envision America being drawn into such a maelstrom.

Life remained somnolent and relatively unchanged in Norwell during these times, with the population still hovering around two thousand. Agriculture, poultry raising and employment in the shoe industry and other small industries still defined our way of life. Residents still looked to the churches as social centers as well as for spiritual fulfillment. There were then four churches within Norwell's borders: First Parish Unitarian on the Hill, the Methodist at Church Hill, the Universalist Church at Assinippi and the nondenominational Union Chapel at Sherman's Corner. In the words of Cap'n Bill Vinal, only Mount Blue remained "unchurched."

It would be another half century before Norwell would have a Roman Catholic parish, but now local Catholics could get to Mass more easily in nearby Scituate or Rockland with the "electrics" running and the wider use of the motor car. No longer did Norwellians of that persuasion have to be "hatch" (baptism), "match" (marriage) and "dispatch" (funeral) practitioners of that faith as had been necessary in the past.

In addition to numerous suppers, whist parties and bazaars, church groups presented original plays, musical revues and minstrel shows.

The Ladies Sewing Circle of the Universalist Church was particularly active at the time; there were no warnings of "hellfire and brimstone" from this church, which believed in salvation for all. Their social events in 1916 included the Seven Cent Social, the Sunshine Club Valentine Party, the Tree Party and the Poverty Social, for which everyone would dress in his oldest clothes with admission being one penny for each letter in the attendant's name.

The Universalists had seen their impressive (1832) edifice burn in 1893. Less than a year later, the present church was dedicated with no mortgage necessary, no doubt due in part to the imagination and fundraising abilities of these ladies. The Assinippi Church was one of the first anywhere to call a woman minister, Reverend Gertrude Roscoe. Accepting the call in 1904, she fully realized that one of her sex would be a curiosity. She did lead the society successfully for several years.

No less active than the adult groups was the Young People's Christian Union of the Church. In May 1916, they presented a farce, *Souvenir Spoons*. In September, their Harvest Festival was a two-day affair with a play, *Too Much of a Good Thing*, and on the following day, a dance featuring a four-piece orchestra. Concurrently, there was an exhibition of fruit, flowers, vegetables and fancy work.

Not to be outdone, the Methodists at Church Hill were equally active. For instance, in April 1916, the Ladies Aid Society had a very successful "Shoe Social," with the admission being a penny for each shoe one owned multiplied by two.

Comparatively, the social slate of the Women's Alliance of the Unitarian Church was rather mundane that year, featuring lunches and suppers and a food sale at the James Library. On a more serious note, the church continued in the tradition of both Samuel May and William Fish, presenting speakers on various social problems. On January 11, 1915, the ladies of Norwell were invited to a lecture on white slavery. The speaker hoped to prevent local young ladies from becoming victims in this "unscrupulous business."

The highlight of Norwell's social calendar was the Masque Ball that was held annually on Washington's birthday (February 11) at Fogg's Hall. In 1914, the munificent sum of $1.50 was the prize for the most elaborate costume—the winner being Geneva Loring Wadsworth—and a like amount to the man with the most grotesque attire. That year, a gentleman attired as an organ grinder and a little boy as a monkey shared the second prize.

From time to time, professional vaudevillians and repertory groups performed at Fogg's Hall and the town hall. The vehicles that pleased audiences the most tended to be westerns and broadly acted melodramas in which the audience had a chance to hiss the villain who comes to foreclose the mortgage, such as in *The Old Homestead*.

A local favorite making many appearances in town was William T. Brown, known as "Comical Brown." The *Rockland Standard* of April 20, 1906, noted that C.E. Smith's group representing the Modern Medicine Company was to perform for several nights at Fogg's Hall. In addition to their performance, they would sell medicines and hold a contest for the most popular lady in town. While performing locally, the actors often stayed at the Turner House on the Hill. Mr. Turner's proud boast was that he had managed to do business in town for many years without serving a drop of liquor.

At that time, weddings and funerals were important parts of the social scene that gave townspeople a chance to get together and also entertain guests from out of town. Most weddings, by today's standards, appear to have been simple affairs. They usually took place in the bride's parlor or in the minister's study, were attended by a small number of guests and were followed by a reception and refreshments of ice cream and bridal cake. Newspaper accounts often detailed gifts received by the couple, ranging from silver and cut glass to parlor, bedroom and dining sets.

Funerals, if not held in church, would be held in the home of the deceased with quite extensive calling hours. Newspapers would summarize the officiating clergyman's remarks, recounting both the virtues and the faults of the dearly departed. Some of the latter could be startlingly candid. Much space was also given to describing the elaborate floral offerings, including the names of the senders.

Also providing social diversion were veteran groups such as the GAR, Women's Relief Corps (WRC) and the Sons of Union Veterans (SUV). More attention to these groups will be given at another time.

Among the summer people particularly, croquet was a popular pastime. This was a sport ladies could engage in even though they were often hobbled by Gibson Girl-style outfits and large picture hats.

No less important during this year were leisure activities pursued in the home and in the country stores scattered throughout the town. Ford's Store at Mount Blue, for instance, had a much-used outdoor bowling alley located in the rear. Cards and board games played both there and in the homes helped wile away long winter evenings before the advent of radio.

Although an early phonograph—the gramophone—was in use, people of all ages liked to gather around the piano in the parlor and sing hymns and the new ragtime songs being turned out by Tin Pan Alley.

The value of all these activities described lessened rural isolation but also, of no less importance, served to break down any social barriers that might have existed. It would seem that the complaint of "nothing to do in this town" would have had no validity in these "good years" before the First World War.

Norwell Flag Day on September 4, 1915. The Norwell Improvement Association provided a flagpole for Norwell Common.

A wonderful float on that gala day in 1915.

Sons of Union Veterans (SUV) on May 24, 1914, dedicate a monument to the Grand Army of the Republic (GAR) at Washington Street Cemetery.

Humphrey Turner, direct descendent of the "Men of Kent," poses at the wheel of his new "machine."

Above left: A series of ads for Norwell businesses during the "Good Years."

Above right: Fun for all on Church Hill!

Universalist Church in Assinippi. The early edifice burned in 1892, and a new one was in place a scant two years later.

Church Hill Methodist Church in 1852. The original St. Andrew's Episcopal Church was located on the hill behind.

PART 4

Two World Wars and a Great Depression

CHAPTER 18

OVER THERE IN FRANCE
AND OVER HERE IN NORWELL

C itizens of Norwell would eagerly await the Boston papers picked up by
Dyer's Express from the late afternoon Greenbush train and distributed
around the town.

Undoubtedly, the headline of June 28, 1914, announcing the assassination
of the Austrian archduke and his wife by a Serbian nationalist would
have created little concern. Of far greater interest would have been the
baseball scores being chalked on the blackboard at the entrances of various
neighborhood stores. Little did most in our small community realize that this
tragedy in a far-off land would result in the United States abandoning more
than a century of tradition of staying neutral in European entanglements.
The murders at Sarajevo triggered the Great War, or the world war of 1914–
1918. The United States would fight on the side of the Allies from April 6,
1917, to the armistice of November 11, 1918.

The struggle would eventually cost 8,000,000 lives, including the lives of
116,000 Americans. In the war, 55 Norwell men and 2 women would serve,
with 17 experiencing the horrors of the western front and 2 being part of the
occupation army in Germany. Unlike the Civil War, which claimed the lives
of 24 South Scituate men, no local doughboy lost his life in the 1917–1918
war. One young man though, William Leslie of Central Street, suffered
severe wounds and the loss of an arm.

The American participation would be unique in that our homeland was
never directly threatened. Also, for the first time in any American war, all
citizens, young and old, would be called upon to help defeat the enemy by

performing war work and making various kinds of sacrifice, some of which involved some loss of personal liberty. A shared sense of sacrifice in time of war defined the era of 1917–1918 in Norwell and throughout the land.

Unlike other recurring crises that had characterized European politics for centuries, the assassination at Sarajevo set off negative forces of nationalism, militarism and imperialism and put into play the alliance system that resulted in most of the major European nations and their colonial dependencies to line up with either the Allies (Britain, France and Italy) or the

Do Your ALL

"DOING YOUR BIT" Is Not Enough

The Fullest Measure of Service

the measure of our personal re-
possibility in this war. Homes
used, families enrolled, resources
opened, waste eliminated means –
MERICA INVINCIBLE.

Every Man, Woman and Child

would think and act and serve together. What each one of us does
uring the next year

Will Decide the Fate of the World

hen each of us learns to sacrifice every
terest in the National Service, Germany's
war will be sealed.

ler in health and efficiency, but without
arrogance and without waste.

ere it an opportunity for each to share
the joy of service, as important as the
rvice rendered by the man at the front.

Save and Lend Your Savings

You can render double service by lending
your savings to Uncle Sam. He need
your savings now. You will need them
after the war, if you keep them till January 1, 1923, you will get your money back
with 4 per cent interest, compounded
quarterly. They may be redeemed before
maturity at any post-office with interest of
about 3 per cent.

Buy War-Savings Stamps

And hold safely the results of your patriotic thrift against a time of need. It help
to win the war. And your dollar will be
more after the war.

They Are Ballots for the Rights of Mankind

A Savings Stamp cost $4.12 in January. 20
to this price one cent has been added for
each month since January. The stamp will
be worth $5.00 on January 1, 1923.

BUY WHERE YOU SEE THIS SIGN

There was great emphasis on the folks at home doing their part to win the war by conserving food and fuel.

Central Power led by Imperial Germany. Americans were shocked to read in the daily papers of Germany's Wilhelm II, "Kaiser Bill," completely ignoring Belgian neutrality as German armies invaded Belgium as the easiest route to Paris and ending the war quickly before the British Expeditionary Force could arrive in France. With Allied propagandists effectively portraying the "savage Hun," hands dripping with blood and bayoneting Belgian children, it was almost impossible to honor President Wilson's plea to be "neutral in thought, word and action."

Among well-known Norwell residents caught in the war zone that summer were former high school principal Mrs. Cox. Also visiting Paris as a fashion buyer was Henry Farrar of West Norwell, who would soon become the fashion editor of the *Ladies Home Journal*. Future president Herbert Hoover, a recently retired mining engineer of forty, was also traveling in Europe that summer. He volunteered his administrative skills and private funds to help fellow citizens, with their assets frozen in European banks, the means to get home.

By 1915, American merchant ships bearing food and material to British ports open to them were attacked by German submarines, defying all the rules of naval warfare. In May 1915, a German U-boat sank British Cunard liner the *Lusitania*, with the loss of 1,200 lives, including those of 128 Americans. Germany claimed the passenger ship was also carrying munitions. Wilson mustered all his diplomatic skills to maintain the peace despite the outrage. Former president Teddy Roosevelt denounced him as "that sissy in the White House afraid to fight." Wilson vowed that he would continue to maintain peace as long as it could be done with honor.

As the debate when on, Norwell observed that September came to be called one of the most important days in Norwell history. An eighty-foot-high flagpole was placed on the common with Senator Henry Cabot Lodge, a close friend of Horace Fogg, as the main speaker. The festivities and the flag waving of that day continued with a baseball game between Kingston and Norwell played at Cushing Field. The memorable day concluded with a concert by Milo Burke's band.

Germany's *Lusitania* pledge to honor the rules of naval warfare was broken with the sinking of American merchant ships, with many carrying munitions. The manufacture of munitions did bring jobs to Norwell residents with George Clark of National Fireworks Company of West Hanover getting a $7 million contract from the Allies.

The presidential election of 1916 featured Democrat Wilson using the slogan, "Re-elect Woodrow Wilson. He kept us out of war." Republican Charles Evans Hughes lost one of the closest elections in American history. Wilson did better in Norwell than previous Democratic presidential candidates. Local voters gave Wilson 107 votes, with Hughes receiving 179. Republican Henry Cabot Lodge easily won reelection. Norwell gave him three times the vote accorded "Honey Fitz" Fitzgerald, President Kennedy's grandfather.

On January 30, 1917, the United States broke off diplomatic relations with Germany because of continued sinking of our ships, since we were a neutral nation. The interception of the Zimmerman Telegram that revealed Germany's conspiracy with Mexico and promised return of California and other territories taken from Mexico by the United States was another factor. On April 2, 1917, Wilson appeared before Congress with a war message highlighted by the words, "We must make the world safe for democracy." Four days later, Congress declared war with few dissenting votes. Even before that date, Miss Maisie Dyer of River Street had enlisted at the Massachusetts Recruiting Station for service as a telephone operator in the event of war.

Two World Wars and a Great Depression

On April 20, 1917, a local public safety committee was formed to coordinate with the Food Administration, the Fuel Administration and other federal agencies. Herbert Hoover, the food administrator, urged Americans to "Hooverize" to observe wheatless, meatless and heatless days. To drink beer or whiskey was to take bread from the mouths of war orphans. Beer drinking diminished also with scorn for beer companies bearing German names such as Pabst and Budweiser. All of this was done voluntarily, unlike during World War II when rationing was instituted.

The *Rockland Standard* reported on a huge patriotic rally held at First Parish that May with Thomas Lawson of Dreamwold as the main speaker. The church was decorated with many flags, including a 150- by 75-foot one owned by Lawson. John Gutterson, the new owner of the Delano Mansion and a talented musician, conducted a patriotic sing-along.

A Norwell auxiliary of the American Red Cross was chartered to better organize blood drives, make bandages and canteen work. The American Boy Scouts, formed nationally in 1910, acquired a Norwell patrol designed to involve young people in war work.

A less positive action in the final analysis was Congress's passage of the Espionage and Sedition Acts. The former allowed suspected enemy collaborators to be deported without due process. The latter made it unlawful to criticize the government in any way. Many people of German ancestry, relatively few in Norwell at that time, anglicized their names in order to ward off hostility. German measles became "liberty measles" and sauerkraut became "liberty cabbage." The teaching of German was outlawed in many schools and symphony orchestras were forbidden to play the music of German composers.

There were five Liberty Loan Drives with rallying posters drawn by illustrators such as Norman Rockwell and James Montgomery Flagg, urging patriots to "give until it hurts," and also using a term from trench warfare, "Go over the top." Norwell residents bought bonds, usually exceeding established quotas. Harry Fogg, treasurer of South Scituate Savings Bank, headed many of these drives emphasizing that every hundred-dollar bond purchased represented one soldier's equipment.

In 1917, Congress enacted a draft act called selective service, using the lottery method unlike the inequitable method of the Civil War in which conscripts could pay three hundred dollars to hire a substitute. District Thirty-eight Draft Board consisted of Norwell, Hanover, Hanson and other nearby towns. An exemption panel was also set up. Many Norwell young men engaged in farm work and vital defense jobs were able to secure exemption. The vanguard of American troops under General John Pershing, commander of the American Expeditionary Force (AEF), arrived in France in the summer of 1917. A staff officer of General Pershing visited the grave of Lafayette shortly after arriving in France and saluted his memory with the words, "Lafayette, we are here." A graduate of Norwell High School in the Class of 1918 titled his honor essay with the same words.

Large numbers of doughboys did not arrive over there in France, the war's principal theater, until the spring of 1918 with the war on the western front stalemated. The opposing armies sat opposite one another in trenches on a front that stretched from the Swiss border to the North Sea. The land between the trenches covered with barbed wire, shell holes and poison gas drifting over all was referred to as "no man's land."

The infusion of American troops was credited with eventually turning the tide for the Allies. Norwell men participated in battles such as the Second Marne, Cantigny, Belleau Wood and the decisive Meuse-Argonne Offensive. Families in Norwell received letters postmarked only "Somewhere in France" for security reasons. Mrs. John Osborne, for one, received word from her son Billy who was fighting with the French army.

In the meantime, a big change came on the home front with the adoption of daylight saving time, effective from the last Sunday in March to the last Sunday in October, permitting more daylight for farmers and war workers.

The war dampened the always-active Norwell social scene, but the traditional masque ball on Washington's birthday was held in 1918 at Fogg's Hall for the benefit of the American Red Cross. With the permission of the Fuel Administration, the ball was to be open until 2:00 a.m.

The increased demand for food brought prosperity to Norwell farms. There was virtually full employment with jobs in munitions and in the shipyards at Quincy and Hingham, which were launching battleships and destroyers in record time. Norwell shoe workers worked overtime in the shoe factories in neighboring towns. For instance, E.T. Wright in Rockland received a government order for 175,000 pairs of shoes.

The guns were finally silenced at the eleventh hour of the eleventh day of the eleventh month of 1918 when the Germans and the other Central Powers agreed to a negotiated peace based upon President Wilson's Fourteen Points.

There was pandemonium of joy all over the world on that first Armistice Day. They were celebrating not only the end of this war but also, because of its sheer horror, the "war that would end all wars."

Norwell celebrated with the ringing of church bells and with a special service held at First Parish with surviving members of the Grand Army of the Republic receiving special recognition.

Two World Wars and a Great Depression

But an unfortunate epilogue to the war was not yet fully played out. In the fall of 1918, the first case of Spanish influenza in the United States was diagnosed at Camp Devens. Before this pandemic was over, ten million deaths were recorded worldwide—more than the total of all the combatants' deaths in the war.

Norwell was not as badly affected as some area communities, but schools and churches were closed and social activities curtailed in the waning months of 1918 and the early part of the following year. Norwell recorded a total of twenty-one deaths in 1918; ten of these were listed as pneumonia induced by the flu. Between January and early February of 1919, four more pneumonia deaths were recorded.

A more uplifting epilogue to the war was the "Welcome Home" event for Norwell servicemen and women, which was held on August 21, 1919. Included in the festivities were a band concert that was conducted by Milo Burke, a fireworks display, and a dance held at Fogg's Hall. Prior to the dance, a supper was served for the returnees and their guests on the grounds of the Seth Foster estate, followed by the presentation of medals to all who had served. Undoubtedly, few could have imagined on that joyous day that in less than a generation there would be another world war necessitating the affixing of Roman numeral I when referring to the world war of 1914–1918.

"MISS MOLLY"

PRESENTED BY THE SENIOR CLASS
OF NORWELL HIGH SCHOOL, FRIDAY
EVENING, MAY 31, AT FOGG'S HALL.

"MISS MOLLY"
CAST OF CHARACTERS

Reginald Peters, a crabbed old man,		Levi Olson
Julian Hewitt, his ward,		Lindsay Ellms
Joe Johnson, his colored servant,		Clifton Lambert
Annie Peters, his twin sister,		Josephine Molla
Molly Peters, his niece,		Veronica Hines
Cissie Saunders, a girl from "Noo York,"		Annie Phair
Pearl White, a colored girl,		Ethel Burns
Lady Elusia Miston, Miss Annie's invited guest,		Marian Boynte

The senior play for the Class of 1918 provided a little lightheartedness in the midst of a war.

119

CHAPTER 19

NORWELL IN THE 1920S

Few decades have had more descriptive appellations attached to them than did the 1920s. The Roaring Twenties, the "Golden Twenties," the Jazz Age and the "Era of Wonderful Nonsense" are just a few. Whether any of these appellations is particularly apt for describing life here in Norwell is debatable.

NORWELL OUT OF THE MAINSTREAM

There are decidedly two ways in which Norwell did not fit into the mainstream. One involves population growth. The federal census of 1920 revealed that for the first time in our history more people lived in urban areas (defined as having more than 2,500 persons per square mile) than in rural areas. Norwell's population still hovered at 2,000. Also, by this date, more than half of the nation's gross national product came from manufacturing. Although there were still a few sawmills and tack and box factories, small farms, wood lots and poultry raising still defined the local economy.

A lighthearted song from the war was "How Are You Going to Keep Them Down on the Farm after They've Seen Paree?" Evidence indicates that most of Norwell's returning doughboys did remain on the farm or, at most, moved to neighboring towns for better job opportunities.

DEDICATION

of the Memorial in Honor of

Norwell's World War Veterans

Saturday, October 7, 1922

at Norwell Common

BAND CONCERT AT 1.30

Thirteenth Regiment Band   H. C. Cushman, Director

DEDICATION EXERCISES AT 2.30

PROGRAM

PRAYER	Rev. Alfred J. Wilson of the First Parish Church
OPENING REMARKS	Horace T. Fogg, Chairman of the Committee
MUSIC	Thirteenth Regiment Band
UNVEILING OF THE TABLET	
	Mrs. Perry H. Osborn, President of the Norwell Chapter, A. L. Auxiliary
REMARKS	Edward M. Sexton, Chairman of the Selectmen
REMARKS	Alan C. Virtue, Commander, Norwell Post, American Legion
MUSIC	Thirteenth Regiment Band
ADDRESS	His Excellency, Channing H. Cox, Gov. of the Commonwealth
ADDRESS	Mayor George G. Moyse of Waltham

Singing of "America" by the audience, accompanied by the Band.

Following the exercises the band will give a concert on the Common.

The committee earnestly request the hearty co-operation of the townspeople in making this day a success.

HORACE T. FOGG
ALAN C. VIRTUE } Committee
ERNEST H. SPARRELL

The dedication of a boulder on the west end of the town common that honored all Norwell World War I veterans.

THOU SHALT AND THOU SHALT NOT

A legacy of the war was two amendments being added to the Constitution: the Eighteenth, forbidding the manufacture and sale of alcoholic beverages, and the Nineteenth, allowing women to vote in national elections. The Eighteenth and its accompanying Volstead Act, the "scofflaw," was flagrantly violated throughout the nation as well as here in Norwell, as subsequent paragraphs will reveal. Norwell women quickly embraced the Nineteenth. Mrs. Isabelle Fogg and other civic-minded ladies made a great effort to get local women registered in time for the 1920 presidential election. When Mrs. Lucy Litchfield, age eighty-nine, registered, she was touted as an example for other ladies to follow. Norwell opted for Harding's "Return to Normalcy" and later, Calvin Coolidge's "Keep Cool with Coolidge" campaign in record numbers.

NORWELL WOMEN AND THE WORLD OF POLITICS

Norwell women's interest in both domestic and world affairs was further demonstrated with the formation of the Norwell Women's Republican Club in 1924, which became a model for female activism throughout the commonwealth. A major early objective was to gain acceptance for women to serve on juries. The ladies of Norwell and surrounding towns heard speakers on subjects ranging from American membership on the World Court and the repayment of the war debts to the Teapot Dome Scandal of the Harding administration.

AMERICAN LEGION POST NO. 192

Returning servicemen were aided in their readjustment by the American Legion, founded in Paris in January 1919, with Norwell Post no. 192 being chartered the following August. Virtually all the local veterans of the late war joined, with their first meeting place being in the Arts and Crafts Building. A committee comprised of Horace Fogg, Alan Virtue and Ernest

Automobiles were a key to the prosperity of the twenties. Families often proudly posed beside their prized possession.

Two World Wars and a Great Depression

Sparrell spearheaded the drive to place a large boulder with a bronze plaque containing the names of all veterans of the world war at the west end of the common. The day of the dedication was October 7, 1922, with Mrs. Perry Osborn, president of the Legion Auxiliary, having the honor of unveiling the monument. An added highlight of the dedication was an address by Channing Cox, governor of the commonwealth.

Members of the American Legion unfailingly turned out for the Memorial Day and Armistice Day parades. The surviving members of the local GAR, now only a handful, were driven in automobiles along the parade route. Increasingly, members of the SUV were taking up the duties of the GAR.

THE FIRST RED SCARE

The end of the war brought a Red Scare, the fear of Soviet Bolsheviks infiltrating the country, often by violent means. There were several incidents of prominent people receiving bombs in the mail, and a bomb went off on Wall Street in September 1920, killing thirty-eight persons and wounding several hundred others. The federal government responded to these events and others by deporting aliens suspected of being radicals. The still unexpired wartime Espionage and Sedition Act was used to stifle free speech in college classrooms and elsewhere. Close to home, a payroll robbery–murder took place in South Braintree, with two Italian radicals being tried, convicted and executed for the crime. Nicola Sacco was a shoe worker from Stoughton and Bartolmeo Vanzetti was a fish peddler from Plymouth. To this day, many feel they were found guilty more because they were Italians and radicals rather than on any strong evidence that they had committed the crimes. The accompanying xenophobia of the Red Scare also brought about the enactment of quota immigration laws unfairly restricting immigration, particularly from southern and eastern Europe.

Late in the preceding year, practically the entire Boston Police Department went out on strike. Most of the public was convinced that Red agitators were behind this and other strikes, rather than low wages that hadn't kept up with the cost of living. Governor Calvin Coolidge called out the National Guard and responded to labor leader Samuel Gompers's plea to restore the striking policemen to their jobs with the words: "There is no right to strike against the public safety by anyone, anywhere, any time."

The *Rockland Standard* of September 11, 1919, reported that people in large expensive cars were seen passing through the streets of Norwell coming from homes at the shore in order to protect their property in the city. Among the state guard units responding to Coolidge was Company A, Fourteenth Regiment, Massachusetts National Guard, which included several Norwell men.

The Klan Reemerges

Acts of still more mayhem against perceived undesirables never occurred in Norwell and surrounding towns despite some rumblings. During its 1920s revival, the Ku Klux Klan directed its venom not only against blacks but also against Jews and Catholics. Members of the Klan made several overtures to town officials in Hanover for permission to hold a rally. None was granted, but, nevertheless, a rally was subsequently held in the woods between West and South Hanover.

In 1924, the pastor of the Church Hill Methodist Church, Reverend Wendell Clark, announced he would give a talk on the Klan presenting both sides of the topic. He found much good in some aspects of the Klan, but he condemned its attitude on the Negro question. During the talk, per the *Standard* account, six "stalwart" young men came into the church, clearly having no sympathy for the Klan. Many members of the parish felt the young cleric exhibited great courage in continuing the talk—that the issue of free speech and free press was at stake. As a postscript, young Reverend Clark did leave the Norwell ministry a short time later with no explanation given as to why.

THE ROCKLAND INDEPENDENT AUGUST 1, 1924

BIG RAID AT NORWELL

Coast Guards and State Cops Give 13 Bootleggers An Un-Lucky Forenoon

There was an abundance of bootleggers in the 1920s.

LOCAL BOOTLEGGING AND RUMRUNNING

There was much flaunting of the Volstead Act within the boundaries of Norwell. So many had few qualms about disobeying the edict that it came to be known as the scofflaw. The North River, with its many coves and high marsh grass, was an ideal locus for rumrunners.

On October 31, 1924, the *Standard* reported that state police and local officers Walter Osborn and Lester West had discovered 950 gallons of Belgian alcohol in the meadow below Union Bridge. It was thought that a rising tide had prevented the miscreants from getting to the outlet where the rum ships were waiting.

On January 5, 1924, five members of the Norwell State Police contingent and a Coast Guard crew from North Scituate surprised thirteen men hiding a cargo of Cuban alcohol at the end of Chittenden Lane. The bootleggers offered no resistance. A five-ton truck was waiting on Forest Street with the stage set for a getaway. Interestingly, it was reported that federal agents that were involved first watched the cabaret show at Chittenden Inn before making their move. Later, two of the inn's owners were also arrested, and their innkeeper's license was taken away.

Other bootlegging operations were uncovered elsewhere in Norwell. On one occasion, a complete moonshine still was found in the swamp off Grove Street. Police chief Walter Osborn and Officer West followed a well-trodden path from the home of the suspect, where they discovered jugs, bottles and a capper before arresting the suspect.

On still another occasion, a flagrantly open operation was discovered at the corner of Main and Bowker Streets when a still was found in the attic of a blazing house. Arrests were made, and the still was confiscated.

NEW QUARTERS FOR THE STATE POLICE

Not as dramatic, but an ongoing crime problem was the prevalence of poultry thefts. These were lessened when a state police unit was located in the town in 1919, first occupying the Arts and Crafts Building and later a modest wooden structure adjacent to the almshouse at the corner of Main and Central. In the early '30s, there was a move to build a modern facility on Route 3 (now Route 53) in North Pembroke. Owing to the influence of Ernest Sparrell, elected to the legislature in 1920, the state police remained in Norwell. The Georgian brick structure at the corner of Main and West Streets was erected in 1935.

THE TURNER HOUSE BURNS

Norwell still had neither a professional police force nor fire department, but in 1921, two volunteer fire companies were established, one at the Hill and the other on Washington Street at Ridge Hill. Not only did this give Norwell a more effective firefighting force, but the Fire Fighters Association and its Ladies Auxiliary also became an important vehicle for building camaraderie among members.

A lead story in the December 3, 1926 issue of the *Rockland Standard* was the burning of the Turner House and an adjacent store on the previous Saturday evening. The former hostelry had become a rooming house and also housed the local telephone exchange. The siren on the roof of the nearby almshouse was sounded, summoning members of the volunteer fire department who were within hearing range.

Unfortunately, the town had minimal firefighting equipment. Most of what they had was the type used in quelling forest fires. With all telephones out, automobiles sped to Hanover, Scituate and Rockland to summon help. The nearby Copper Corner Brook was full, and hoses were laid down. Another fortunate circumstance was only a light breeze was blowing from the southwest. Otherwise, homes and businesses in the immediate vicinity could have been wiped out. Although the Turner House was gone, the fire proved to be a wake-up call, and town meetings in successive years appropriated money for fire apparatus. Farsighted citizens also talked of the need for laying down a townwide water system.

THE NORWELL VISITING NURSE ASSOCIATION

Still another major step forward was a growing concern for better medical services. In 1924, the state medical board cited the town for not having a resident physician to minister to the needs of the community. The last local physician had been Dr. Harry Little, who had moved to California in 1913. The town's immediate rejoinder to the criticism was to point out there were a number of physicians among Norwell's summer residents. It was also argued that Scituate, Rockland and Hanover had a proven track record for responding to medical emergencies in a timely manner.

Norwell was in the forefront medically by having a very effective Visiting Nurse Association (VNA), which was established in 1921. The immediate impetus for its establishment was not only the influenza epidemic of 1918–

1919, but it was also because of the tragic deaths in 1920 of three children in the Bates family—ages four, five and six—of scarlet fever, whooping cough and measles over a three-week period. Mrs. Amy Sylvester was the VNA's first president.

On March 10, 1921, by an almost unanimous vote, the town appropriated $1,200 for a district nurse. That summer, proceeds from the Norwell food booth at the Marshfield Fair were used to purchase a Ford Runabout for the nurse. A well-baby clinic was set up, and a dental clinic was established in the schools. Pupils received instruction on better sanitary procedures, and each classroom was outfitted with emergency medical supplies.

NORWELL SPORTS

Also adding to the wellness of Norwell's children and young adults was a particularly active sports scene in the decade. In the country as a whole, the twenties were known as a golden age of sports, dominated by such icons as Ruth, Gehrig, Grange and Tunney.

The Union Athletic Association (UAA) purchased Ridge Hill Grove in 1921. The earlier reports of the Grove's inevitable demise when the trolleys ceased running proved to be erroneous. The UAA had begun in 1916 with meetings in the early years being held in the North Hanover Fire Station. Many Norwell members had previously been active in the Norwell Baseball Association.

Famous teams such as the Colored Philadelphia Giants and the bearded House of David were favorites. Satchel Page was one of those who played in the field.

Changing times would bring a decline in the Grove following World War II, and in 1955, the Grove was sold to the town with a payment of $1 to soon become the site of a new elementary school.

In 1924, Norwell's annual town meeting considered the adoption of the state act permitting Sunday sports. Among those speaking in favor of the petition by the UAA were James Barnard, William Leonard and Ernest Sparrell. Horace Fogg, backed by John Gutterson, countered with a plea for maintaining the quiet of the Sabbath. The final vote was seventy in favor and fifty-eight opposed. Mr. Fogg then presented a motion that would require those attending Sunday games to get a certificate from the selectmen saying they had attended Sunday services. The Reverend Alfred Wilson quickly ensured the defeat of this motion saying he wanted no unwilling listeners at his services.

With a new high school opening in 1922, a more diversified sports program became possible. Norwell High's basketball squad was champion of the South Shore League in 1926 and in 1927. They ended the season with twelve wins and two losses. Norwell had a girls team as well, and both teams played against larger schools such as Bridgewater, Rockland, Randolph and Scituate, as well as those with similar enrollments such as Duxbury and Hanover.

FLAMING YOUTH

Before turning the page on the 1920s, one might wonder if our somewhat staid community tolerated flappers—the liberated females of the time who wore skirts that reached well above the knee and bobbed their hair in a boyish style. They and their boyfriends smoked, drank in speak-easies, danced the Charleston, parked in lovers lanes and generally embraced a hedonistic lifestyle.

How many Norwell young women, if any, embraced this mode of living is, of course, impossible to say. But a dress and hairstyle, which in the early twenties went against a prevailing sense of decency, soon became the norm. Norwell High School's yearbook, the *Shipbuilder*, for the mid- and late-twenties, reveals that many young ladies had adopted the flapper hair and dress style, and in their minds, looked like the "cat's meow." Not to be outdone, some of the young men posed for their senior photos emulating the slicked, pompadour hairstyle popularized by filmdom's current heartthrob, Rudolph Valentino.

Norwell High and Grammar School was built in 1922 in the rear of the town hall. Both buildings burned in 1935.

DENOUEMENT

Many historians of fashion maintain that in good times, like the twenties, skirt lengths go up, and in dire economic times, they go down again. This was decidedly the case in the twenties and in the decade to follow. Norwell voters had heartedly endorsed Coolidge prosperity and Hoover's prediction that poverty was about to be banished from our land for all time. But just how real was what appeared to be unparalleled prosperity? Did most of the wealth belong to too few people at the top? Had the manufacture of radios, electric refrigerators, vacuum cleaners and automobiles, often purchased on the installment plan, outrun the public's ability to consume? And what about the mania for buying stock on margin, with the expectation that the bull market would go on and on?

Norwell, along with the rest of the nation, would receive the answer in October 1929 when the market crashed and the country plunged into the worst economic depression in its history. In 1930, radio crooner Rudy Vallee introduced a song that became the theme of the early thirties—"Brother, Can You Spare a Dime?" The majority of Norwell folk, so the record speaks, had few dimes to spare.

CHAPTER 20

NORWELL IN THE 1930S

COPING WITH THE GREAT DEPRESSION

O n October 29, 1929, the stock market collapsed, or as *Variety* magazine put it, "Wall Street Lays an Egg."

There is no record of Norwell's more economically favored jumping out of hotel windows, but surely their stock portfolios had shrunk considerably. A year later, the Rockland Standard editorialized as follows: "A long period of good times leads to extravagance, indifference, laziness, discourtesy, conceit, and shiftfulness. The biggest fools are the first to be hit. Their thinly marginized stocks and real estate are sold for what they will bring." While banks throughout the country collapsed as the 1930s progressed, banking in Norwell remained strong. Treasurer Herbert Robbins of the South Scituate Savings Bank, only the fourth treasurer in its nearly century of existence, announced that deposits at the bank had increased by $79,471.28 in the previous year.

But this did not present the full picture of the town's economic health as the effects of the stock market collapse spread to the "cells and capillaries" of the American economy. The pages of the *Rockland Standard*, particularly in the early years of the decade, are full of notices of bank foreclosures on Norwell homes and businesses. The September 8, 1932 edition contains thirty-two notices from the Norwell tax collector that property in tax arrears would be sold at public auction. On the other hand, a social item of that year details the marriage of the daughter of one of our summer people with a reception for five hundred at the Copley Plaza.

President Hoover correctly recognized that the Depression was worldwide in its scope and stated his belief that it was part of the natural economic cycle and would pass without undue interference by government. His pronouncement that "prosperity is just around the corner" soon had a hollow ring as unemployment reached 25 percent of the nation's labor force. When a person considers that many of those employed were working only part time, the situation appears still worse. Hoover, the great humanitarian of World War I, quickly became the most unpopular man in America. Added to the national jargon were phrases such as the "Hoover Depression," "Hoovervilles" (encampments of unemployed living in tents and other substandard structures) and "Hoover blankets" (newspapers stuffed inside one's clothing for warmth). His reputation reached its lowest point when he used the army and tear gas to rout unemployed World War I veterans who had come to Washington to petition Congress for immediate payment of a bonus that had been promised for the future.

THE NORWELL WORKFORCE IN 1930

According to the 1930 federal census, farm labor (148) was still the top occupation in Norwell, followed by various types of service jobs in private families (56). Twenty-seven individuals were employed as rubber mill workers in West Hanover and 26 were employed in shoe factories. Other top occupations included poultry, carpentry, auto mechanic and road building. The automobile had become such an important part of life that these two last occupations remained strong throughout the 1930s. As humorist Will Rogers put it: "America would be the only nation in the history of the world to go to the poor house in an automobile." In fact, more people owned automobiles than had bathtubs. This didn't seem to be such an anomaly to a midwestern farm wife who pointed out that you couldn't go to town in a bathtub.

The fact that so many Norwell people still worked so close to the soil meant that even in these harsh economic times they were able to put food on the table. However, those working in factories, particularly the shoe factories, were hard hit by the worsening depression. Tourists passing through the town had often wondered how, even in the best of times, Norwell folks supported themselves. Many locals were forced to show high levels of ingenuity. When the Cunard liner *Laconia* sailed from Boston in September 1933, it carried six hundred pounds of apples from the Old Pound Orchard off Green and Pleasant Streets. Perry Osborn trucked them in. Also on South Street, a hen house six hundred feet long with three floors was being built to house

4,500 laying hens. Obviously, Norwell people were heeding Franklin Delano
Roosevelt's advice not to be paralyzed by fear.

In the same week that FDR delivered the first of his "fireside chats" over
the radio, the Ladies Auxiliary of American Legion Post no. 192 sponsored
a musical revue called *Better Times*. Participants sang: "Old Man Grouch and
Pessimist have been banished by Frivolity and his partner Hope."

NORWELL VOTES IN THE 1930S

In 1932, Democrats nominated Governor Franklin Delano Roosevelt of New
York for president. The Republicans nominated incumbent Herbert Hoover.
Roosevelt campaigned on behalf of the "forgotten man" and promised a
New Deal without many specifics as to what it would entail other than a
pledge to balance the budget. Hoover pointed to his public works programs
to create jobs and his program to lend money to failing banks and businesses
with hope that prosperity would thus "trickle down." His programs were
derided by the Democrats as being "too little, too late."

There is ample evidence that substantial numbers of Norwell people
were very seriously affected by the Depression, such as the previously noted
mortgage foreclosures and properties being sold for delinquent taxes. Relief
efforts were being left to private agencies and local governments, which
were soon overwhelmed by the magnitude of their task. In May 1932,
the American Red Cross released one hundred bags of flour for Norwell
residents. The town meeting of 1932 appropriated the unprecedented sum
of $6,500 for welfare in addition to $2,300 for the infirmary. Surprisingly,
these difficulties did not translate into a local landslide for Roosevelt, despite
his huge tallies nationally. In that year, Norwell cast 592 votes for Hoover
and Curtis; the Roosevelt and Garner local vote was 153—pretty close to
four to one for Hoover.

FDR began his administration by declaring a "bank holiday" that
provided needed confidence in the banks that had survived. FDR and his
Democratic majority in Congress experimented with various programs
in an effort to provide relief and bring about recovery. If one approach
failed, they would try another. A casualty of all this experimentation was
a balanced budget. In 1936, Franklin "Deficit" Roosevelt asked voters if
they were better off than they had been four years earlier. The answer was
a resounding "yes" nationally; Roosevelt and Garner received 523 electoral
votes to only eight for the Landon–Knox ticket. Despite some improvement

in the local economy, the vote in Norwell was 672 for Landon and 180 for FDR—again close to four to one for the Republicans.

Did the vast majority of Norwell voters resent the enlarged powers assumed by FDR? Did they see him as a threat to the old Yankee tradition of rugged individualism?

FURTHER SIGNS OF RECOVERY

In April 1933, National Fireworks Company of West Hanover announced they would reopen. Unlike during World War I, the company would now manufacture pyrotechnics for celebrating the Fourth of July. Other good news was the announcement that business was picking up at the Salmond Tack Factory, and that they were now employing twelve. Small restaurants, tearooms and overnight cabins began to spring up on Washington Street. Mrs. Mary Cheever, mother of the author, opened a gift shop on Washington Street. It was reported that Julia Wheeler had acquired much new merchandise for her gift and yarn shop. Still more good news was that Joseph Tolman planned to expand his poultry operation with forty additional acres. At the time, he had 6,000 to 7,000 laying hens. A record had been set: 56,000 eggs, with 4,250 chickens hatched. He now had five full-time employees plus his three sons working at the plant.

One of the most ingenious ways of beating the Depression occurred at Walter Johnson's across from the Norwell House where he owned a log cabin and twelve acres. Johnson had thirty-six adult minks with the expectation of having a population in excess of one hundred for the coming breeding season. Even on those grim days of Depression, Mr. Johnson was willing to gamble that a market for mink coats would exist.

NORWELL: WET OR DRY?

FDR's theme song, "Happy Days Are Here Again," gained added resonance on December 5, 1933, when Utah became the requisite thirty-sixth state to ratify the Twenty-first Amendment, which repealed the Eighteenth and thus relegating the Volstead Act to the "ashcan of history." But "dry" sentiments going back to the Cold Water Army days of Reverend Samuel May and the temperance efforts of Reverend William Fish (1865–1885) remained strong.

True, Norwell had had its share of scofflaw adherents during the nearly fourteen years of national Prohibition. The *Rockland Standard* reported one of the last raids on October 13, 1932, when Norwell, Rockland and state police raided a seventy-five-gallon still on Grove Street. The still was dismantled and taken to the state police barracks.

In a local referendum in 1938, Norwell reverted somewhat to its temperance past when citizens voted 440 to 284 to exclude the sale of alcoholic beverages. The exclusion of malt beverages prevailed by only two votes and not granting package store licenses carried by only twenty-one votes.

MUSIC, LITERATURE, THEATER AND OTHER LEISURE-TIME PURSUITS

During these Depression years, Norwell continued to provide much of its own entertainment with church groups, veterans' groups and the schools leading the way. Whist parties, suppers, minstrel and variety shows and dramatic productions were plentiful. Several plays were presented in the stable loft converted into an auditorium at the Samuel Deane place. The celebration of Washington's birthday on February 22 had long been a tradition in Norwell. A George Washington fete with scenes from the life of our first president was presented on the grounds of the Fogg estate. Since the thirties were the heyday of the big bands, several Norwell young men formed orchestras and were entertaining at dances being held throughout the South Shore.

A local poet of note was Mrs. Gleason Archer of Church Hill, wife of the Suffolk Law School dean, who published several volumes of poetry containing many poems extolling the beauty of the North River Valley. Also of special note was a new edition of Shakespeare's *A Midsummer Night's Dream* with introduction and notes by Pauline Leonard of Washington Street, who was a student of Elizabethan literature and formerly a librarian at West Virginia University. One of the attractive illustrations was a fairy scene from a production given on the grounds of the Fogg estate in 1926.

A favorite holiday in New England had always been Thanksgiving, and 1939 was the year that we had two "turkey days." President Roosevelt had proclaimed the third Thursday of November rather than the last Thursday, hoping that an earlier Thanksgiving would lengthen the Christmas shopping period and provide an economic boon. There was such an outcry over this breach of tradition that Governor Saltonstall proclaimed an added

Thanksgiving on the traditional date. This provided a boon to local turkey raisers who sold turkeys to families observing both dates. The following year and thereafter, Thanksgiving returned to its traditional date.

NORWELL LOOKS TO THE FEDERAL GOVERNMENT

During the early period of the Great Depression, private charitable organizations such as the Red Cross and local charities, tried to alleviate the suffering of those in need. But the scope of the Depression was so great that these groups were soon overwhelmed. With the coming of the New Deal, myriad programs such as the Works Progress Administration (WPA), Public Works Administration (PWA) and the Civilian Conservation Corps (CCC) provided immediate relief and attempted to bring about economic recovery.

Another one of these agencies was the Civil Works Administration (CWA) with Herbert Lincoln as local administrator. One hundred and sixty-three Norwell men and women applied for work, mostly for painting and

In the early thirties, the birthplace of Sarah Kent, mother of L. Vernon Briggs, was moved from the corner of Bowker and Grove Streets to Norwell Center. It is now owned and maintained by the First Parish of Norwell.

forestry work. Project no. 610 called for the remodeling and painting of Center Primary School. Local officials now stressed that henceforth welfare dependents of the town will consist of only those physically unable to work. Prejudice against federal funds appears to be one reason why Norwell voters turned down a grant of $102,000 under the Federal Relief Act of 1935, which was 45 percent of the estimated total that was needed to greatly improve the town's water situation. Firefighters and real estate people were not pleased by the town's action.

Local families (in which the father was without a job) were receiving letters from their sons in CCC camps throughout the country. In addition to food, shelter and clothing, these young men were paid thirty dollars per month, twenty-five dollars of which had to be sent home. Although federal funds were not applied for in the building of a new high school, WPA (referred to by critics as "We Poke Along") funds were applied for doing grounds work and building athletic fields for the new school. WPA funds also provided a workforce for cleaning up after the 1938 hurricane and other disasters. New Deal programs such as the WPA had been phased out by 1942; obviously, with jobs created by wartime economy, there was no further need for them.

THREE NEW IMPOSING EDIFICES

In the 1930s, Norwell saw two public buildings fall victim to fire, and two others became victims of the wrecking ball. The town hall and the high school annex burned in December 1935. (Construction of the new high school will be discussed in full in a subsequent chapter.) At about the same time, the almshouse closed its doors. A much more enlightened and economically practical mode of dealing with the local indigent was adopted. The board of selectmen ordered that an auction of the infirmary's effects be held. Included in the sale to the highest bidder would be the facility's cow and a flock of hens. The small wooden building near the almshouse formerly housing the state police was also razed.

NEW STATE POLICE BARRACKS

In 1935, the state began the construction of six new substations, with one of these to be constructed at the head of West Street. That the substation remained in Norwell was largely due to the tireless work of Ernest Sparrell.

Two World Wars and a Great Depression

In October 1933, it had been announced that the state police would leave Norwell for a $35,000 station on Route 3 (now Route 53) in either Hanover or North Pembroke, a decision that was later rescinded, allowing it to remain in Norwell. Arguing that the station should be placed on a major artery is a position still heard today, over seventy years later.

CUSHING HALL

A major gift came to the town of Norwell with a provision in the will of Miss Florence Cushing, a member of the first graduating class at Vassar College and longtime summer resident. She provided $100,000 to be spent for building a large edifice to be used either as a town house or a primary school to be located within the radius of a half mile from First Parish Church. Another stipulation was that the windows of the church be replicated in the new structure. The gift was in memory of her father, Hayward Peirce Cushing, and her uncle, Nathan Cushing. Among her other bequests were $10,000 to First Parish Church in memory of Jane Peirce Cushing and $5,000 to the William Fish Fund to benefit the James Library.

Since the almshouse had been razed and the wooden state police barracks had been replaced by the new brick structure across the road, the corner of Main and Central Streets was chosen as the site of Cushing Memorial Town Hall. Ralph Harrington Doane was selected as architect with a plan calling for a brick building using the Georgian colonial style. In addition to the main hall and stage, there were a number of smaller office areas provided. A special feature was a large fireproof vault for the safekeeping of town records. The completed edifice was dedicated on November 2, 1936.

After fire destroyed the existing town hall in December 1935 and with the opening of the new, Norwell reverted to its colonial roots by holding its town meeting in First Parish (Meeting House) Church. Since all vestiges of theocracy had disappeared by the early nineteenth century, selectmen decided it would be unseemly to have voting take place in the church. Therefore, they decided to use the GAR Hall on High Street for that purpose, which also served as a concession to people living in the west end of town.

THE HURRICANE OF SEPTEMBER 21, 1938

A challenge of another sort occurred on this date. Weather forecasters were caught completely off guard by the hurricane that ripped into Long Island and then caused a tidal wave that left downtown Providence under six feet of water before slamming into Massachusetts and then onward into northern New England and Canada. The hurricane hit the South Shore at about 4:00 in the afternoon with sustained wind velocities of over one hundred miles per hour for several hours. The *Rockland Standard* described Norwell as a scene of devastation with scores of enormous trees being uprooted, including a century-old fir in front of the tomb yard at First Parish Cemetery. The selectmen, the tree warden and the highway surveyor helped people reach their homes that evening. Their wives and daughters were on the phones taking news of damage. Most roads and highways were cleared of wires and trees by 11:00 p.m. A special town meeting of October 10, 1938, voted $975 in emergency funds, which would cover the cost of removing trees from the highways. Cleanup continued for months, providing jobs for WPA crews.

THE WORLD OF TOMORROW?

On April 30, 1939—the sesquicentennial of Washington's inauguration as president in New York City—the New York World's Fair opened at Flushing Meadow. With its futuristic symbols, the Trylon and the Perisphere, the exposition promoted "The World of Tomorrow." This was the fair that many Norwellians, now in their seventies, and older remember attending. But before the fair closed for the season, German armies had invaded Poland on September 1, 1939, and the twenty-year armistice had come to an end. Both Britain and France came to the aid of Poland a few days later. Little did most Americans realize that the United States would be at war in two years' time. War production would create full employment, bringing the country out of the Depression, something that eight years of the New Deal had failed to do. However, the most lasting legacy of the 1930s would be major reforms such as regulations of banks and stock market, increased rights for the working man and woman and, above all, the Social Security Act of 1935, which provided a safety net for the aged, the unemployed, the disabled and dependent children.

CHAPTER 21

NORWELL WELCOMES A
NEW HIGH SCHOOL

In 1888, the year of South Scituate's decision to change its name to Norwell, town meeting first appropriated funds to provide a high school education for its young people. Until 1896, high school classes were held on the second story of the Grange Hall on Main Street. From 1896 to 1922, high school classes were held in the town hall, which was adjacent to the present town hall. In 1922, a separate high school addition was added to the town hall building.

In October 1935, selectmen named a building committee to oversee the construction of a badly needed addition to the school and a new heating system. Plans were made to accept funds from the Federal Emergency Relief Appropriation of 1935. Ironically, just two months later, the town hall and high school were completely destroyed by fire. The state fire marshal's report blamed faulty wiring. Norwell students displaced by the fire attended afternoon sessions in Hanover.

A special town meeting was held on January 6, 1936, with a building committee named. One of the members, A. Ralph Gordon, called for the town to reject any federal monies saying, "Someday I believe there will be a little honor roll of American communities who refuse to depend on outside funds. I hope this town will be one of these."

It was later in 1936 that Franklin Delano Roosevelt and his New Deal received a resounding national endorsement, with Roosevelt winning a landslide with all but two of the forty-eight states. Many Norwell citizens, however, turned a "thumbs down" on Roosevelt and voted for Republican

Alfred Landon in that election, by a ratio of four to one. Landon believed the New Deal was wasteful and a challenge to individual liberty. The "Landon slide" in Norwell was all the more remarkable in that many Norwell citizens benefited by the New Deal's work relief programs. The town agreed not to apply for federal funds for their new school, thereby making a strong statement against a "something for nothing" philosophy many felt characterized the New Deal.

Another preliminary decision made was the matter of location. Land formerly owned by the family of William Penn Brooks was selected at a purchase price of $30,000. Still another decision was to fireproof the building at an additional cost of $10,000. Ultimately, about $130,000 was appropriated. Work began on May 15, 1936, with R.H. Doane as the architect and Irving P. Rocheford as contractor. Just one year later, the school opened with 225 students in grades five through twelve.

On Thursday, May 6, 1937, an article about the new school got front-page billing in the *Rockland Standard/Rockland Independent* newspaper.

What today is known as the Sparrell Building, named for Nellie Litchfield Sparrell, who served on the school committee for several decades, provided space for Norwell's secondary school needs until 1961. After that, it was an elementary school for more than forty years.

Today, after recently completed extensive renovations to provide public school offices and space for Norwell Historical Society Archives, it stands as resplendent as it did in 1937 when it represented a symbol of Norwell's commitment to public education, even in the darkest days of the Great Depression.

Norwell's high school opened in 1937, looking as resplendent today as it did in the 1930s.

CHAPTER 22

FRIDAY NIGHT AND
SATURDAY ON ROCKLAND HILL

In the 1930s, Norwell still had many small neighborhood stores where residents could buy meat and groceries for everyday needs. Peddlers hawking sundry goods, such as articles of clothing, sewing supplies and small hardware items, were still traversing the roads and byways of the town. The Spinning Wheel at Queen Anne's Corner, or Julia Wheeler's as it was then called, was without peer for knitting and craft supplies.

But longtime Norwell residents who are now senior citizens remember Rockland Hill (in Rockland) as the major shopping mecca for the entire South Shore. Union Street, from the depot at the south and extending for nearly a mile northward, was lined with an incredible array of shops. There were also businesses spilling onto neighboring streets. There was diagonal parking on both sides of Union Street, and three policemen were needed to direct traffic on weekends.

Rockland Hill had three major supermarkets and numerous produce and meat markets. Specialty shops, such as millenaries, furriers, perfumeries and tobacconists, did a brisk business, along with three pharmacies, three hardware stores and several stores specializing in stationery, magazines and books. Department stores offering men's, women's and children's clothing were available in all price ranges.

The most venerable of these was Rice's Department Store at the corner of Pacific Street; it was a true emporium in every sense of the word. Mary Knapp of Norwell recalls the pneumatic device by which your money and sales slip were sent to a second-story office and a tube containing your

Norwell citizens were among those who thronged Rockland Hill in the 1930s. Rockland Hill was the shopping mecca for the entire South Shore.

change and sales receipt was sent down. Another memorable stop for the small fry was Lelyveld's Shoes, where they could view the bones of their feet by stepping into an X-ray machine.

Other favorite stops in Rockland Hill might be W.T. Grant's for a bag of freshly roasted peanuts from the peanut machine or stopping by the candy counter at Woolworth's, where it was a tough decision to decide between the nonpareils or the ice-cream drops. Perhaps an afternoon or evening in town would be capped off with a bite at McNeil's Sandwich Shop or an ice-cream soda or a "college ice" at George's. Unlike in Norwell, there were a number of taverns operating on the street. Young children wondered why the owners never washed their large plate-glass windows.

Norwell had no movie theater until one operated at Queen Anne's Plaza during the 1970s, so most movie-goers went to the Strand Theater in Rockland, which changed its program three times a week. Friday and Saturday's show was geared to children with a western and a breathtaking serial thrown in. For ten cents' admission for children, and a quarter for adults, one could view the feature, the co-feature, the newsreel, previews of coming attractions and a short subject or two. Wednesday was "dish night," when you received a piece of dinnerware (Depression glass) with each admission. In time, one might assemble a whole set. Also in the bargain

Two World Wars and a Great Depression

It was a wonder of the modern age. Children were thrilled to view X-rays of their feet at Lelyveld's Shoes on Rockland Hill.

was a chance to forget the Depression for a few hours while watching Fred and Ginger, the adventures of Robin Hood, a Busby Berkeley musical or a Shirley Temple feature.

Norwell was a great town to live in for its quiet and bucolic scenery, but Rockland was the big city.

Our older citizens still have fond memories of when all roads led to Rockland Hill on Friday night and Saturday in the days of their youth.

CHAPTER 23

NORWELL'S GREATEST GENERATION FACES WORLD WAR II

1939–1945

THE WORLD SETTING: 1931-1939

On Armistice Day, November 11, 1938, songstress Kate Smith reintroduced on her radio show a song that composer Irving Berlin had quickly withdrawn from a World War I army show as a failed effort. For this occasion, Berlin had written a new opening stanza for "God Bless America": "While the war clouds gather far across the sea, let us all swear allegiance to a land that is free."

The song now perfectly captured the mood of the nation over a deteriorating world situation and a confidence that America's ultimate response would be the correct one.

As British prime minister Neville Chamberlain's appeasement at Munich had only whetted Adolf Hitler's appetite for further territorial demands; as Benito Mussolini completed his conquest of Ethiopia; and as Japanese bombs continued to rain down upon China, a contentious debate went on in Congress and throughout the nation between the isolationists ("America Firsters") and the interventionists. Over the following years, all the way up to Pearl Harbor, the vast majority of Americans agreed with the hero Charles Lindbergh that American vital interests were not at stake. Most were convinced that our involvement in the "war to end all wars" in 1917 to 1918 had been a mistake.

World War II began on September 1, 1939, with Hitler's invasion of Poland. His blitzkreig attacks continued, resulting in the rapid collapse of

UNITED STATES
OF AMERICA

War Ration Book One

WARNING

1 Punishments ranging as high as *Ten Years' Imprisonment or $10,000 Fine, or Both*, may be imposed under United States Statutes for violations thereof arising out of infractions of Rationing Orders and Regulations.

2 This book must not be transferred. It must be held and used only by or on behalf of the person to whom it has been issued, and anyone presenting it thereby represents to the Office of Price Administration, an agency of the United States Government, that it is being so held and so used. For any misuse of this book it may be taken from the holder by the Office of Price Administration.

3 In the event either of the departure from the United States of the person to whom this book is issued, or his or her death, the book must be surrendered in accordance with the Regulations.

4 Any person finding a lost book must deliver it promptly to the nearest Ration Board.

OFFICE OF PRICE ADMINISTRATION

No: 296568 -282

Mrs. Osborn's war ration book. Housewives had to deal not only with food shortages but also with ration coupons.

nations such as Holland, Norway, Belgium, Denmark and France in the spring of 1940. Britain now stood alone with new Prime Minister Winston Churchill, who could only offer "blood, sweat, toil and tears" as the British nation and commonwealth appeared to be doomed.

Each morning, between the weather forecast of E.B. Rideout and Carl Moore's *Breakfast Club*, Norwell radio listeners heard the sound of air-raid sirens, bombs exploding and the answering flak of artillery amid the static of the short-wave radio. Many of our older citizens may remember Edward R. Murrow's broadcasts from London as Britain fought for survival during the "Blitz," a time Churchill called Britain's "finest hour." In January 1941, there was a rally for British relief sponsored by the Church Hill Improvement Society. A British refugee speaker called for support for the afflicted people and introduced two British sailors rescued from a ship badly damaged in a fight with the German cruiser *Bismarck*.

FDR ELECTED TO A THIRD TERM

How Norwell Benefited by the Breakdown of American Neutrality

In 1940, FDR defied tradition by running for and being elected to a third term. Although he beat Republican Wendell Wilkie in a national landslide, Norwell voters opted for Wilkie over FDR by a margin of three to one. In the midst of the campaign, Congress, with Roosevelt's backing, enacted the first peacetime draft, maintaining that "in a free society, the obligations and privileges of military training should be shared generally in accordance with a fair and just system." The local draft board consisted of nine towns: Norwell, Cohasset, Scituate, Hanover, Marshfield, Pembroke, Hanson, Duxbury and Halifax. The first numbers were drawn and physicals taken. Frank DiFabio was the first Norwell man to receive "greetings" from his friends and neighbors after being designated 1-A. The American Legion and Legion Auxiliary sponsored a reception for him at Cushing Hall before he left for boot camp. He was presented with many gifts including a jackknife wrapped in currency.

In March 1941, Congress took a major step toward abandoning neutrality by passing the Lend Lease Act that gave the Allies "all aid short of war." This essentially ended the problem of being able to secure employment. National Fireworks Company in West Hanover had turned from producing pyrotechnics to munitions. Both the Hingham and Fore River Shipyards expanded greatly. The 1930s had brought a decline in both marriages and the birth rate. When the defense boom began in the summer of 1940, virtually ending the Depression, couples no longer had to defer marriage and having a family. The vital statistics in Norwell town reports beginning at this time decidedly bore this out.

NORWELL "GETS A LEG UP" WITH TWO NEW MILITARY INSTALLATIONS

In February 1941, ten months prior to America's entry into the war, A. Ralph Gordon, local chairman of the Massachusetts Committee of Public Safety, began enrolling volunteers for nonmilitary duty. He remarked, "It isn't necessary to smell smoke before you have a fire drill."

In April, Secretary of the Treasury Henry Morgenthau announced that United States Savings Bonds would go on sale at local post offices. For example, $18.75 for a bond would yield $25.00 in ten years, an annual return of 2.9 percent. One could also purchase savings stamps for $0.10, $0.50 and $1.00.

In July, the Norwell Committee for Public Safety made an appeal for aluminum, which netted 886 pounds locally. In August, residents heard that preliminary work had begun on the Weymouth Naval Air Station on land taken from Weymouth, Rockland and Abington. It would soon become a common sight to see large dirigibles, then referred to as blimps and fueled with helium gas, floating over the town as they engaged in German U-boat reconnaissance. In August 1945, local residents would witness one of these blimps go down on Maple Street at the Norwell–Scituate line during a thunderstorm.

On July 31, 1941, the *Rockland Standard* reported that word had been received that seven and a half square miles of land lying in the towns of Norwell,

"Don't You Know There's a War On?" To save paper, correspondence was done via "V-Mail" (Victory Mail).

Hingham, Cohasset and Scituate would be taken by the navy for ammunition storage. In Norwell, Mount Hope Street and the northern end of Prospect Street would be affected. Also, the far end of Mount Blue Street would be dead-ended.

In September, recruiting tables were set up at Cushing Hall for the Defense Committee. Forty-five air-raid wardens were duly recruited. The Women's Defense Committee, however, faced a problem in that many more women wanted to be in motor transport than in canteen work.

On the last Armistice Day prior to America's entry into the war, Norwell hosted the tri-town parade. Among the marchers were fifty Civil Defense women, Boy Scouts with a float containing a short-wave radio setup and representatives from the Norwell Grange on a farm wagon containing a large cornucopia proclaiming "Food Will Win the War."

A "Date That Will Live in Infamy" and its Immediate Aftermath

It is now close to seventy years ago, but most of those still alive remember exactly what they were doing on that Sunday afternoon when they first heard the news of the Japanese attack on Pearl Harbor. In his war message the following day, President Roosevelt spoke of "Sunday, December 7, 1941, a date which will live in infamy." Word was received from two Norwell boys stationed in Hawaii that they were safe. Theodore Dyer Jr. was stationed at Hickham Field, and George Strachan was at Wheeler Field.

All sympathy for isolationism seemingly vanished overnight. As seen in earlier paragraphs, the Norwell home front was in full preparedness mode. One way to gauge the patriotism of the time is the activity at military recruitment stations during the days following the Japanese sneak attack. Still another way is to review the discography just after Peat Harbor. Within days, songs like "We Did It Before, and We'll Do It Again," "Coming In On a Wing and a Prayer" and "Let's Remember Pearl Harbor" were being played everywhere.

There were record-breaking movie audiences during the war years. Since Sunday drives were out for the duration, a good substitute was taking in a movie. People shared rides to get to the Strand in Rockland and the Playhouse at Scituate Harbor. As many as a third of the movies produced in Hollywood at that time had war themes. Among the films advertised in the Standard during those years were *Bataan*, *Guadalcanal Diary*, *Crash Drive*, *Air Force*, *The Flying Tigers*, *Thirty Seconds Over Tokyo*, *A Walk in the Sun* and two featuring a future president, *Desperate Journey* and *This is the Army*. Sandwiched between the "B" movie and the feature, one could get a glimpse of the "real" war with the newsreel, *The Eyes and Ears of the World*.

NORWELL REPRESENTED IN ALL COMBAT THEATERS

In one of his major earlier addresses, President Roosevelt had said, "To some generations much is given. From other generations much is expected." The generation that came of age in the '30s and '40s not only had to endure a deep economic depression but also the hardship of nearly four years of global war. No wonder broadcaster Tom Brokaw referred to them as the "greatest generation." Two hundred and thirty-three individuals from Norwell served in World War II. Included in this number are ten local women who either served as nurses or in the newly organized women branches, the WACS and the WAVES. One Norwell couple, Mr. and Mrs. Archie Merritt, displayed a three-star service flag in their window for their three sons, servicemen Raymond, Emerson and Warren. Citizens placed pins on the map of the world where loved ones were serving, bearing exotic names such as El Alamein, Anzio, Salerno, Bataan, Guadalcanal, the Burma Road, Normandy, Bastogne and so forth.

In August 1944, the sad news would be received that Samuel Turner Jr. had been killed "somewhere in France." That July, word had also come that Carleton Ryder, a former social studies teacher at Norwell High, had been killed in the invasion of France. While teaching in Norwell, he and his wife had resided at Jacob Lakes Shore.

THE HOME FRONT RESPONDS

On December 9, 1941, just two days following Pearl Harbor, word spread throughout the town that an enemy plane had been seen approaching the Atlantic coast. Both Fore River and National Fireworks were evacuated. Two hours later, the sighting was labeled a false alarm.

A meeting was called by the Norwell Defense School for male volunteers to serve as additional air raid wardens and as enemy aircraft spotters. Amazingly, 350 of the 400 adult males in town responded. The United States attorney general ordered all aliens (noncitizens) to surrender any cameras and radio sets they might have. If this appeared to be a violation of civil rights, far worse was the order forcing the evacuation of 110,000

Americans of Japanese descent living on the West Coast to internment camps in Nevada and Wyoming.

On March 24, 1942, Hanover and Norwell had a twenty-minute trial blackout following regulations of Governor Saltonstall.

Two wartime federal agencies that affected everyone were the War Production Board (WPB), which limited nonmilitary production, and the Office of the Price Administration (OPA), which established price controls. In 1942, all the social clubs in Norwell suspended meetings for the duration in order to curtail unnecessary driving and heating. However, in 1943, President Roosevelt urged local lecture platforms, such as the Norwell Women's Republican Club, to resume activities. He said, "In time of crisis, they give citizens the facts they need to know."

The Norwell Tire Rationing Board was set up amid reports from around the town that thieves were removing wheels from automobiles for tires. Prior to sugar being rationed in April 1942, Sargent's, a popular eatery in Assinippi, was offering ten cents a pound for all the sugar they could get. In May, gasoline rationing was put into effect. Pleasure driving became nonexistent as most citizens received "A" coupons that allowed the purchase of a mere three gallons per week. All home-to-work drivers were required to carry three additional passengers to qualify for supplemental mileage.

Local rationing boards allotted rationing booklets containing coupons (points) that were used to purchase meat, canned goods, shoes and so forth. The age, health and whether a family member was employed in war work determined the number of points received. Norwell public school teachers offered their services in setting up the rationing system.

Since Norwell was so close to the coast and with two shipyards, an air base, an ammunition depot and a munitions plant all nearby, strict federal blackout and dim out restrictions were put in place by Alan Virtue of the Norwell Auxiliary Police. Dark out coverings for windows had to be lowered at dusk and one half of each car's headlights had to be painted black. A sad consequence of this latter regulation was large numbers of cats and dogs being killed on the roads.

With shortages of cloth, the length of women's skirts was regulated by the War Production Board. Men's trousers were made without cuffs and what had been the hallmark of a well-dressed man, the vest, was eliminated. Ladies had loved their nylon stockings with the introduction of that fabric in 1940. Since nylon was now being used in making parachutes, all nylon production for nonmilitary use ended. Some women responded by using a cosmetic paint to simulate nylons.

WORKING AROUND THE CLOCK

With so many defense plants and shipyards operating at full tilt, unemployment was almost nonexistent. For instance, at the height of the war, the Hingham Shipyard employed five thousand workers, and Fore River ten thousand. Norwell workers at Hingham were among those who built landing ship tanks (LSTs) and later destroyer escorts. Launched at Fore River in Quincy were battleships such as the *Massachusetts*, heavy and light cruisers and aircraft carriers such as the *Lexington*.

Doing more than her bit for the war effort was Caryl Ringe (Mrs. Wilder Gaudette) of Central Street. In 1941, she secured the position of assistant secretary to the general manager of Bethlehem Steel's Quincy yard. In 1942, Bethlehem Steel transferred Caryl to Hingham where she served as private secretary to Sam Wakeman, general manager of the Hingham Shipyard. At the close of the war in 1945, Mr. Wakeman became general manager at Quincy with Caryl serving as administrative assistant to Mr. Wakeman then and for many years thereafter.

Although still called National Fireworks Company, the West Hanover plant expanded its munitions making by taking over Clark's Airport. In 1943, the *Rockland Standard* carried a large ad calling for evening (swing shift) and midnight (graveyard) shift workers. The ad read, "We want women who can load shells." Among those loading shells was Helen Fogg, daughter of one of Norwell's wealthiest men. Fireworks workers could be easily identified around town as their skins took on a dark yellow hue from the sulfur they were exposed to. When thousands of workers at West Hanover went off their jobs protesting bad labor conditions, the American Federation of Labor threatened male workers with loss of defense work deferment and being classified I-A for the draft if they didn't go back. With full production resumed, the *Standard* was able to report in July 1943 that National Fireworks Company had become the largest munitions plant in the world!

With more women joining the workforce than ever before, "Rosie the Riveter" was being featured in War Information Bureau posters. It even became acceptable for women to wear trousers on the job. Additionally, movie star Veronica Lake, known for her long "peek-a-boo" hairstyle, cut her hair short as an example for female defense workers that long hair could be dangerous on the assembly line.

Norwell School Children Do Their Part

Norwell school children were in the vanguard of those collecting scrap metal. Norwell and Pembroke were reported to be in a "dead heat" working for the Massachusetts title for scrap iron collection. Two ancient water turbines that had lain in the mud in Third Herring Brook for eighty years were turned in.

Pupils were encouraged to plant "victory gardens" and to engage in war-related opportunities such as the Norwell Social Service Committee that in 1943 packed between 170 and 180 Christmas boxes for men and women. Each box contained a copy of *Reader's Digest* with a year's subscription, toilet articles, writing paper, cards and a cribbage board. Individual schools staged competitions for the highest percent of purchases of war stamps and bonds each week. In the seventh War Bond Drive, students and other townspeople purchased a total of $383,000 in stamps and bonds, 200 percent of the quota.

One change in the high-school curriculum motivated by the war was a course in aeronautics. In most respects, high school life went on as normally as possible, but it became difficult to maintain interscholastic athletic schedules with the gasoline limitations. Also, because of the paper shortage, the graduation classes of '43, '44 and '45 were unable to publish yearbooks. Some male seniors in good academic standing were allowed to leave school at midyear (still being able to receive their diplomas) in order to join the service or begin college studies.

Upper-class, high-school girls and other Norwell young ladies accompanied Charles Baldwin of Central Street, a well-known square-dance caller, to Camp Edwards on the cape where Mr. Baldwin served as director of social dancing.

Passing of Joseph Foster Merritt

In August 1944, relatives and friends gathered in First Parish Church to pay respects to Joseph Foster Merritt, Norwell's town clerk for forty years and author of *History of South Scituate Norwell, Massachusetts*, published in 1938. A portion of Reverend Alfred Wilson's tribute follows: "He will be remembered for his fidelity to principle, for his loyalty to his community. Here on this hill is the place where he did the things for which he will be remembered."

Lieutenant Tedeschi Missing in Action

In the waning months of the war, word was received that Lieutenant Ralph Tedeschi was missing in action in France. Good news followed on March 15, 1945, that Tedeschi had been freed from a German prison camp by advancing Soviet troops. The *Rockland Standard* article went on to report that letters received from him in prison camp had shown that he was "unbowed by adversity." The later article concluded with this comment: "His attitude was always of that quality that causes him to be remembered most pleasantly." Ralph Tedeschi did not come to reside in Norwell until the early 1960s, but the well-known supermarket entrepreneur became a notable Norwell benefactor. His estate, Tara, built on land formerly owned by the Tolmans, would become the scene of many townwide festivities such as Norwell's celebration of our nation's bicentennial in 1976 and the celebration of Norwell's centennial in 1988.

Death of FDR

Norwell folks along with people the world over were shocked upon hearing the news coming from Warm Springs, Georgia, on the late afternoon of April 12, 1945, that the president had died. It has become obvious when reviewed in retrospect that, despite what doctors had said and carefully doctored campaign photos, voters had essentially elected a dying man to an unprecedented fourth term as president. Now, the burdens and decisions involving war and the coming peace were in the hands of a little-known former senator from Missouri. Most agreed that Harry S. Truman was no Roosevelt but fervently hoped he could meet the challenges lying before him.

V-E Day and V-J Day

All the jubilation over victory in Europe, V-E Day on May 8, 1945, was somewhat tempered by the realization that the Pacific war was far from over. The Japanese had exhibited a fierce fanaticism at Iwo Jima and in their kamikaze strikes, and as they would in the upcoming Okinawa campaign. Most pundits estimated that the war would go on for another year and a half with an invasion of the home islands before Japan would surrender. But August 6, 1945, brought an atomic bomb to Hiroshima, with another one dropping on Nagasaki three days later.

A Narrative of South Scituate/Norwell (1849–1963)

At 7 o'clock eastern wartime, August 14, 1945, President Truman announced that victory over Japan had been achieved. One modification of the unconditional surrender ultimatum was allowing the Japanese emperor to reign but not rule, providing he renounced his divinity status. After three years, eight months and seven days, World War II had passed into history.

When news of the Japanese surrender was heard in Norwell, crowds gathered all over town. Church bells rang out, automobile drivers sounded their horns. Vendors of balloons, flags and noisemakers appeared with their wares, and spontaneous celebrations went on into the wee hours of the following day. Peace would indeed be wonderful.

PART 5

A Time of Rapid Change

CHAPTER 24

THE EMERGENCE OF A SUBURB

1945–1963

POSTWAR AMERICA IN ITS WORLD SETTING

There was little doubt in anyone's mind that the United States had emerged from World War II as the world's strongest power.

The United States had been the "great arsenal of democracy" and was now the sole possessor of the atomic bomb. There was great confidence that American participation in the newly created United Nations would preclude still another world war that the old League of Nations, minus American participation, had earlier failed to prevent. Also, it was fervently hoped that the awfulness of Hiroshima and Nagasaki would make future war unthinkable. There was confidence that the power of the atom, if placed under civilian control, could be a force for good.

The apprehension that the nation, without a military production economy, might return to a state of economic depression never materialized because of a number of factors. Among them were an unprecedented level of wartime savings accompanied by a pent-up demand to replace prewar automobiles, washing machines, refrigerators and other consumer goods. Also, with the baby boom beginning in 1946, there was a growing housing shortage.

Late in the war, Congress had passed the Serviceman's Readjustment Act, popularly called the GI Bill of Rights. Under this legislation, veterans desiring a college education or even training in the trades could receive tuition grants and also a monthly living allowance. A college education, long out of reach for most of the middle class, now became a reality. Norwell did its part of helping returning veterans adjust to civilian life by allocating funds for the Norwell Service Center. Many veterans wishing to ease their way back into civilian life became members of the "52-20 Club." They were able to receive weekly checks of twenty dollars for an entire year. At this time, it was a manageable living wage for a single person.

Still another feature of the GI Bill was the provision allowing veterans to obtain mortgages at a low rate of interest. The consequences of this latter provision would be enormous for Norwell.

NORWELL EMERGING FROM THE WAR

Norwell servicemen and women returned to a community little altered from the one they had left a few years earlier. Population had risen modestly to just under 2,200, but the town was still a place others passed through, perhaps buying vegetables from farm stands such as "Breezy Bend," as they traveled to the Cape or to nearby shore towns. But in the succeeding fifteen years, population would rise to more than 5,000, and the town would be forced to deal with long-avoided issues such as water supply, police and fire protection and a more up-to-date school system.

The Eisenhower Highway Program would result in vastly improved access to Boston and to sites of developing industries along the Route 128 corridor. By1961, the Southeast Expressway would have extended as far as Derby Street in Hingham with plans to complete the final eleven miles to Duxbury. In addition to the interchange at Derby Street, a second at Hingham Street in Rockland and a third at Washington Street in Hanover, near "Dead Man's Curve," were planned. These three links would position Norwell for still greater population and commercial growth in the coming years.

Previous to the war, the only housing development worthy of the name had been Jacob Lake Shores, which was built in the late 1930s. In the immediate postwar years came Norwell Homes off the western end of Grove Street. These homes were generally built on lots measuring one-sixth of an acre. With the first zoning regulations in Norwell enacted in 1941, questions of the validity of these and other early zoning regulations arose over whether there was a quorum present at town meeting or whether a voice vote was legal. When the Washington Park subdivision was begun in 1951, the size of the lots had risen to between eight thousand and twelve thousand square feet.

There was so much controversy over zoning at this point that moderator Herbert Lincoln resigned his position so he could better fight zoning from the town meeting floor. There was also an ongoing philosophical debate. Typical of this was a statement by Donald Wilder from the floor of town meeting. He maintained, "I am firmly convinced that I have no right to tell you what to do; also, you have no right to tell me what to do." Obviously, rugged individualism was still alive and well in the town of Norwell.

By the time the Ridge Hill subdivision was built in the 1950s, half-acre requirements were in place. In the next decade came the Barque Hill development, which would receive national kudos for its careful siting of large colonials and capes built on one-acre, integrated landscaped lots. There were walking paths, open spaces and the preservation of historic sites connected with the glory days of North River shipbuilding.

It was difficult to determine which of the three major needs facing postwar Norwell—water, schools and public safety—needed to be dealt with first as they were so interrelated. Many citizens were worried that these expensive projects could result in transforming Norwell from a rural community to a suburban "bedroom" town. In an article appearing in the *Rockland Standard* at the time, William G. Vinal bemoaned what Norwell might lose with words containing more than a hint of sarcasm: "Look at the ads for today's homes in Norwell. They do not say how many potatoes you can raise but about scenic advantages, recreational facilities and cultural attractions. Even the red maples are being held idle to open in anticipation of suburban developers and the almighty dollar."

"Water, Water Everywhere and Not a Drop to Drink"

This area of the country experienced several serious drought years in the late 1940s and in the 1950s. A 1949 *Standard* editorial pointed out the irony of Norwell residents living in homes with every modern convenience yet having to obtain drinking water from the "never failing spring" in the town field off River Street. In 1957, Norwell firemen would be called upon to deliver water to the nearly 50 percent of Norwell homes where wells had gone dry. It would become increasingly apparent that for both health and safety reasons the state could no longer ignore Norwell's lack of municipal water.

The following are some items from the *Rockland Standard* during these years highlighting steps Norwell was finally taking to identify water sources and to lay down pipes and bring water to all sections of the town:

A Time of Rapid Change

August 28, 1948, "Norwell Awaits New Water System": $47,500 appropriated to begin construction in Church Hill and Ridge Hill areas.

July 28, 1949, "And So Wonder Came to Light": Hanover water was turned into new water mains on High and Grove Streets.

February 15, 1951: Water service currently installed in five miles of streets, although Norwell still appears years away from full installation.

March 21, 1951: Town meeting, by a vote of 271–0, appropriated $28,000 for laying mains in the Jacob Lake Shore area.

July 8, 1954: Hanover says it can't continue to supply Norwell with water. The agreement with Hanover allowed 50,000 gallons a day. On a recent hot Sunday, 110,000 gallons were used. J. Lee Turner, chairman of the water commissioners, said the town was actively prospecting for its own water. Three areas were being looked at, with two off Pleasant Street in the Wildcat area.

July 28, 1955: Norwell Board of Health announced it would not approve future housing developments in areas not reached by town water. The town was still getting all of its water from Hanover.

September 5, 1955: Town approved bond issue of $528,000 for water. State would reimburse the town for half.

November 8, 1956: Hanover serves notice that they will not supply any more water after December 31, 1957.

February 21, 1957: J. Lee Turner announced the good news that a well was found on the west side of Pleasant Street. The well was then equipped with a 350 GPM electric pump and an auxiliary diesel engine. In the first six months, 30 million gallons of water were pumped. Money was appropriated for purchase of necessary land, erection of a standpipe, erection of a pumphouse and for installation of five miles of mains. River Street would now have town water.

Although far from completely solved, the preceding data shows that in a ten-year period, Norwell had made great strides in its goal of bringing a reliable water supply to all of its citizens.

Schools, Schools and More Schools

In the decade and a half following the end of World War II, the Norwell Public School System took great leaps forward. The first of the baby boomers, arriving in 1946, began affecting school enrollments by the early and mid-1950s. The school census of 1947 counted 328 children enrolled in our schools. By 1960, the school population had nearly quadrupled, with 1,252 young people in the schools.

With school enrollments on the rise everywhere and an attendant shortage of trained teachers, the state minimum salary for teachers rose to $2,500 a year in 1953. Norwell had been paying beginning teachers considerably less. Local teachers also had to contend with overcrowded classrooms and shortages of textbooks and other supplies. A major source of contention locally was not whether new facilities were needed but where new schools should be located—should they be all in a central part of town to prevent divisions or in various neighborhoods?

In 1949, the town decided to build a new elementary school in the geographical center of the town at a cost of $375,000. The state would pick up half the tab, with the money being returned over a twenty-year period. The new central school was dedicated on February 22, 1950. Later, it would be named for a former principal, Ella Osborn, and still later would become the Norwell Town Hall.

In 1952, a $300,000 addition to the high school was voted upon. It contained seven classrooms, a mechanical drawing room and a home economics room. In January 1954, the resulting "Sparrell Wing," recognizing longtime school committee member and town clerk Nellie Sparrell, was opened with facilities for pupils in grades six, seven and eight.

In October 1954, Superintendent Clifton Bradley, after studying population trends and enrollment projections, voiced his opposition to a regional high school that would include Hanover. Norwell Town Meeting voted in agreement with Bradley's position by a considerable margin, while Hanover voted in favor of a regional school.

With school enrollments steadily rising and a population explosion in the Ridge Hill–Grove Street area, there was talk of building a new school in that part of town. Paving the way for this was the abandonment of the old Ridge Hill School situated at the juncture of Washington and Oak Streets. In 1954, the Union Athletic Association turned over Ridge Hill Grove to the town for a new school, receiving a payment of one dollar.

The Norwell Taxpayers Association voiced their opposition, not only because the school would not be centrally located, but also because it would be directly in the line of flight patterns from Weymouth Naval Air Station. With the projection of there being 110 first-graders in four classrooms and continued population growth, particularly in that part of town, the building of the school went forward. It opened on January 2, 1956, bearing the name of Grace Farrar Cole, a longtime teacher and school committee member who had recently died.

A Time of Rapid Change

In 1957, the William Gould Vinal School was built on Old Oaken Bucket Road and named in honor of Professor Vinal.

In 1958, six rooms were added to the Osborn School, and in that same year, a high school planning and building committee was appointed and charged with site selection and engaging an architect.

Two additional factors other than population growth moved the town to continue upgrading the schools. One was the dismay felt when the Soviets launched the space satellite Sputnik. The other was the publication of *American High School Today* by James Bryant Conant, former president of Harvard and President Dwight Eisenhower appointee as high commissioner in Germany. Conant, an expert on atomic energy, advocated an upgrading of lab facilities and of instruction in math and science. Congress responded with the first of the National Defense Education Acts. Local superintendent Bradley warned that in the rush to close the missile gap, the teaching of the humanities should not be neglected. The new high school opened for students in September 1961. This was the facility located behind the Sparrell Building that later served as the junior high school only to be demolished a few years ago with the building of the Goldman Middle School.

In 1962, the regional superintendency composed of Norwell, Hanover and Hanson was dissolved with the permission of the legislature. Frederick Small, who had been serving both as high school principal and assistant superintendent, became superintendent of the now fully independent school system of Norwell.

POLICE, FIRE AND CIVIL DEFENSE

A third long-neglected issue was the matter of police and fire protection for a rapidly growing community. A part-time auxiliary police force maintaining law and order, no matter how conscientious, had become an anachronism for a town of Norwell's size. At a special town meeting on September 12, 1955, citizens voted to provide the town with "a permanent man with adequate transportation." Selectmen promptly named Kenneth Bradeen as our first professional chief of police. In his first annual report, Chief Bradeen emphasized his effort to minimize the department's budget but, at the same time, presented specifications for an ambulance cruiser. In addition, he called for the appointment of a special officer for daytime work.

In his second annual report (1956), he listed the total budget of the department as $4,500.00, of which $4,032.50 constituted his own salary.

A permanent officer, Ted Baldwin, was added to assist in controlling "hot rodding," investigating breaks and so forth.

By 1961, there were four permanent men in addition to the chief: Baldwin, George Cavanaugh, Richard Joseph and Ellsworth Keene, along with a contingent of special police officers and auxiliary officers. In 1960, town meeting provided funds for a Police, Fire and Civil Defense Communication Center. Part-time persons answering calls were paid eighty-five cents an hour, which was raised to a dollar an hour in March 1961.

Throughout the fifties and for a time thereafter, fire protection was still handled in the time-honored way of volunteer fire companies directed by a board of fire engineers with an appointed chief. The number of fire stations had been reduced to three: Norwell Center, Ridge Hill and Church Hill.

Finally, in this most contentious period of the cold war, Norwell possessed a strong civil defense committee under the direction of W. Clarke Atwater.

THE "SILENT GENERATION"

Before moving on to further discussion of strictly local events of the 1950s, a brief glimpse of America and the wider world would be in order. Following World War II, our nation remained at peace just short of five years. On the last Sunday in June of 1950, Communist forces of North Korea crossed the Thirty-eighth Parallel, invading the Republic of South Korea. The United States lent support to the United Nations police action to repel the invasion. A total of 133 Norwell residents were to serve in the Korean Conflict, now often referred to as the "forgotten war." President Truman's attempt to limit the scope of the war by not involving Red China led to his dismissal in April 1951 of Supreme Commander Douglas MacArthur for failing to follow orders. This involved the constitutional mandate of civilian (presidential) control over the military. MacArthur returned home for the first time in fourteen years and delivered a speech before Congress, outlining his position and ending with his memorable farewell: "Old soldiers never die; they just fade away."

There were cries from many quarters that impeachment charges should be brought against Truman. The president earlier had gained bipartisan support for his leadership in containing the spread of Communism with the Truman Doctrine, the Marshall Plan and his support for NATO. His 1948 upset victory over Republican Thomas Dewey had not only negated the country's faith in political polls, but it had defied history with Truman as candidate of one part of a three-way split in the Democratic Party. As usual, in that era, Norwell voters opted for the Republican, Thomas Dewey, by a margin of nearly four to one.

As the 1952 presidential election approached, it appeared inevitable that the Democrats' twenty-year hold on the White House would come to an end with Dwight Eisenhower as the Republican nominee. On March 25, 1952, a large rally was held in Norwell under the direction of John Bond, president of the Norwell Eisenhower Club. He had secured as the main speaker Christian Herter, a future Massachusetts governor and American secretary of state.

Eisenhower's pledge, "I will go to Korea," implying that he would honorably end the unpopular war, was a big factor in his easy victory over Adlai Stevenson. Norwell voters endorsed the slogan, "I like Ike," giving him four times the vote accorded Stevenson. In 1956, "I like Ike even better," carried him to victory by even wider pluralities, both locally and nationally.

The decade of the fifties has been referred to as the "fabulous fifties" for many reasons, the chief of which was the unparalleled prosperity of the decade. Home ownership and automobile ownership reached record highs. Televisions were brought into nearly every living room, while the question persisted whether it would remain the "boob tube" or become a force for positive good in disseminating information and culture.

But the fifties had a darker side that had often been overlooked. One pundit has referred to the fifties as "the time of the buttoned-down collar (conveying the dress-for-success values and the buttoned-up lip)." It was a time when many of this "silent generation" kept their convictions to themselves out of fear that they might be viewed as a "Red" or a "Pinko." School teachers and other public employees were required to take loyalty oaths as a condition of employment. This national paranoia was abetted by witch hunts, most notably by Senator Joseph McCarthy, who investigated perceived Communist influence and security risks in the state department, in the arts and academia and in the military, with little regard for individual rights. It was during the Army–McCarthy hearings that McCarthy's roughshod methods were exposed in full view of enraptured television audiences by counsel for the army, Attorney Joseph Welch of Boston.

A look at several forums held in Norwell also reveals the temper of the times. In February 1950, the Norwell Women's Republican Club had as their speaker Robert Welch, a Cambridge businessman who criticized huge waste in Washington created by overlapping departments. Later, Robert Welch would become the founder of the ultraconservative John Birch Society. In

May 1956, the Turner Legion Post presented a talk by John Glades, an undercover agent for the FBI who had posed as a communist for five years.

Peripatetic Helen Fogg, a staff member for the Unitarian Service Committee, gave a talk at Cushing Hall titled, "Eyewitness Report on Life in Europe Today." Dr. Kirtley Mather, professor of geology at Harvard, addressed the local Republican ladies on "Atomic Energy in Peace and War." Norwell's William Gould Vinal presented a slide talk before the Norwell Historical Society on a recent trip to Europe in which he detailed resistance to the UN there. He found the people of Europe to be "restless, furtive, suspicious, and generally wishing to be left alone."

Just before he left the White House in 1961, Eisenhower addressed Congress and the nation on the dangers posed by the "military-industrial complex." Although there had been crises in Vietnam, the offshore islands of Formosa, in Suez, in Hungary and in Lebanon, partial solutions had been found that did not involve American fighting men. He had also moved forward on assuring racial equality, largely through his naming Earl Warren as chief justice. In 1954, the Warren court unanimously ruled in *Brown v. Board of Education of Topeka* that "separate was inherently unequal." When local officials in Little Rock tried to prevent black children from enrolling in white schools, Eisenhower sent troops to enforce the law.

In 1960, Massachusetts had the opportunity for sending a native son to the White House for the first time since John Quincy Adams. The race between Massachusetts senator John F. Kennedy and Richard Nixon was stunningly close nationally but not here in Norwell. Here, Nixon received nearly twice the vote accorded Kennedy.

CHAPTER 25

A STILL EMERGING COMMUNITY

A PRELUDE TO A NEW AGE

The following are some items from the *Rockland Standard* highlighting Norwell events:

September 6, 1945, "Wife-Savers, Inc.": Frozen Foods Locker enterprise was allowed by the zoning board of appeals to use the garage of the W.D. Turner property (the old parsonage at 761 Main Street). The outside of the building was to be redecorated to be more pleasing to the eye as one rides the main street of Norwell.

November 28, 1945, "Death of Ernest Sparrell at Age of 73": Mr. Sparrell was a longtime funeral director, community activist and a member of the state legislature from 1920 through 1936. As a state representative, he served as chairman of the Committee on Highways and Bridges. He was also remembered as the president of the Marshfield Fair Association from 1930 through 1943. A testament of his prominence and respect for his character was his funeral service at First Parish, which was attended by Senator Saltonstall, Governor Tobin and Lieutenant Governor Bradford.

May 20, 1948, "Return of Samuel Turner, Jr.": Norwell Legion Post 192 met the flag-draped casket of Samuel Turner Jr. at Greenbush upon his return from France. After lying in state at Cushing Hall, his body was interred in Washington Street Cemetery. The local post would thereafter be called Samuel Turner Jr. American Legion Post 192.

April 21, 1949, "Norwell Women's Republican Club Observes Twenty-fifth Anniversary": The club now had a membership of one thousand from Norwell

OPEN HOUSE!

WIFE SAVERS

LOCKER PLANT

MAIN ST., NORWELL

Will Be Open For Your Inspection

Sun., June 2, 1946—10 a.m. to 9 p.m.

Modern Locker Plant

CUSTOM PROCESSING—SHARP FREEZING

Full Line of FROZEN FOODS ON SALE

Distributors for Home Freezers and Supplies

(LOCKERS)   (BULK STORAGE)

A zoning variance allowed this short-lived business.

and surrounding communities. An early objective of founding members had been to gain the right for women to serve on juries in superior court, which was achieved in 1951 when nine Norwell women were drawn for duty: one secretary, one housewife and seven "at home."

April 30, 1950, "Archbishop Richard Cushing Establishes Catholic Parish in Norwell": The founding pastor, Reverend Norbert McInness, initially ministered to about seventy-five families using the Grange Hall on Main Street as their first place of worship. The archdiocese then purchased the present rectory and a few outlying buildings on Washington Street. One of these was transformed into a simple church and dedicated to St. Helen. The present edifice was built in 1962 under the direction of Reverend John Kenney, with the earlier church becoming St. Helen's Hall.

October 1, 1953, "Norwell High School Has a Reunion for All Classes": The family of Attorney Herbert Lincoln could claim three generations of graduates, with his mother Mabel Pinkham being in the first graduating class in 1891 and with he and his two daughters being subsequent graduates.

January 28, 1954, "Norwell's Convoluted Telephone and Mail Service": Norwell residents were served by four telephone exchanges: Hanover, Rockland, Scituate and Norwell. At this time, there was a section of River Street where the residential address was Norwell, the mail address RFD Rockland and the telephone was Hanover, but you had to say "Taylor" if you wanted to use the phone. If your house was on fire, you had to call Rockland to reach the Norwell fire chief. The tax collector had to place a toll call to reach most voters. Mail delivery was impossible. Sending a letter from one end of Grove Street to another meant that the letter first had to go three miles to Greenbush for a postmark.

March 4, 1954, "John C. Bond of Norwell Purchases *Rockland Standard* and *South Shore News*."

April 14, 1955, "Developer Joseph Gould Buys the Former Henry Norwell House and Sixty-Five Adjoining Acres": Ultimately, he would build many homes on Norwell Avenue and Trout Brook Lane on the former Norwell property.

April 14, 1955, "Tree Farm Established at Town Field on River Street": Tree warden Wesley Osborne Jr. predicted that few of the nine hundred remaining elm trees in town would have survived in ten years. Consequently, he planted hearty varieties such as crimson red maples and sugar maples that would be ready to transplant in two or three years.

May 19, 1955, "Salk Vaccine Administered in Schools Under Direction of Board of Health and Dr. Raymond Vinal": Parents held the right to request no vaccination. The last major polio outbreak was to occur in the late summer of 1955 with two local children dying; the opening of school was delayed for two weeks.

"Cap'n Bill" Vinal, an advocate for our environment.

March 22, 1956, St. Patrick's Day blizzard: This was the storm in which the Italian frigate *Etrusco* went aground in Scituate. A record number of automobiles passed through this town loaded with people wishing to witness the sight.

August 14, 1958, "Norwell Selectmen Vote to Keep One Central Post Office in Norwell Center": Just a few years earlier, mail was being delivered from seven different post offices.

June 18, 1959, "Goodbye Old Colony": *Standard* writer maintained the time had come, and that it would not be missed, just as the horse and trolley were not missed. (In 2007, the train returned to Greenbush.)

October 20, 1960, "Union Bridge": Union Bridge Bill received legislative approval to completely build the bridge. Earlier, Norwell had favored only repair work.

September 7, 1961, "Civil Defense Urged to Build Fallout Shelters": This was a time of major confrontation over Berlin between the United States and the Soviet Union. One of the more sophisticated of these shelters was built at the home of Jean Mayborn and Doug Marshall on River Street.

October and November 1961: Efforts by Norwell to convince the state to depress the expressway as it moved through Norwell got nowhere. The announcement was made that the Hanover–Norwell link would be ready by November 1963. The Southeast Expressway Development Commission presented a rosy picture of the area's future economic advantages.

"Professor Vinal Take a Bow"

No account of Norwell in the decade and a half under discussion would be complete without again highlighting what William Gould Vinal, now an energetic octogenarian, had accomplished for the town and, for that matter, the whole area. It was Cap'n Bill's voice warning through the years of the need to protect one of the region's most precious commodities from being destroyed if pollution from the town's upriver was not controlled.

A culmination of years of effort by Vinal was securing Black Pond and twenty-five adjoining acres as the first nature conservancy site in New England. Also, he can receive credit for placing Norwell in the vanguard of towns following through on legislation allowing cities and towns to establish conservation commissions.

In addition, Vinal's persistence and logical arguments resulted in the South Shore Nature Center's being located on land abutting Jacobs Pond and woodland and fields bequeathed by Dr. Henry Barton Jacobs to the

A Time of Rapid Change

Preservation of New England Antiquities. The center has remained a "hands-on" nature classroom for young and old alike.

The following are portions of a laudatory editorial appearing in the *Rockland Standard* on March 16, 1961, titled "Professor Vinal Take a Bow."

> *Town Meeting action which established conservation commissions in five South Shore towns is a tribute to the efforts of Professor William G. Vinal of Norwell. For years he has sought to awaken our burgeoning communities to the dangers of creeping expansion which could very well destroy the rich natural heritage of the South Shore.*
>
> *Of first importance, we believe, is the North River Valley. We say this because the valley meanders through all five towns, is still largely in its natural state, and offers a wealth of opportunity for land and water recreation. Before too much of the shore line is gobbled up by developers, it may be possible for the five conservation commissions to get together in a cooperative effort to preserve the last salt river valley which is so important historically and so rich in nature's gifts to mankind.*

William Gould Vinal, "Cap'n Bill"

Emeritus Professor of Nature Education

University Massachusetts at Amherst

An inscription in Cap'n Bill's book to Edward Rowe Snow of Marshfield, a maritime historian. Note Vinal's characteristic signature with the teepee.

A Vinehall Publication

Norwell, Massachusetts

1958

NORWELL AT THE BEGINNING OF A NEW ERA

As Norwell entered the decade of the nineteen sixties, steady population growth with its attendant needs went on unabated. The sixties and seventies were also decades that made many less idealistic with its assassinations, race riots, a missile crisis in Cuba, an unpopular war in Vietnam, and a country shaken by a profound distrust in the veracity and integrity of our president; with the crimes relating to Watergate.

In 1961, the nation's youngest elected president proclaimed in his inaugural address that "the torch has passed to a new generation of Americans." Increasingly in Norwell, too, the responsibility of balancing growth with the commitment of maintaining Norwell's singular rural charm would pass to a new generation of Norwell leaders. In this first decade of the 21st century, one need only look around to see how well they have taken up that charge.

PART 6

Appendix

CHAPTER 26

ROCK-RIBBED REPUBLICANS

1920–1944

Ninety years ago this past August, Tennessee became the thirty-sixth state, the number constitutionally required to ratify the Nineteenth Amendment, giving all American women the right to vote in the coming presidential election of 1920.

That fall, public-spirited Isabelle Faulkner Fogg, who was the wife of Horace Fogg, visited all the ladies in Norwell, urging them to exercise their franchise. Over the next twenty-four years, there would be seven presidential elections during alternating periods of boom and bust and during alternating times of uneasy neutrality and global war. Norwell voters, however, remained politically constant, revealing much about the town, the character of its people and how they met the challenges of the times.

In 1920, there was a resounding landslide for "back to normalcy with Harding" and an even bigger landslide locally. The vote for Republican Harding was 409 with 48 for James Cox, his Democratic challenger—a ratio close to nine to one. What Harding meant by normalcy was that progressive reform and international involvement had been overdone by the outgoing Wilson administration. In 1924, Norwell voters opted to "keep cool with Coolidge," again by a ratio of about nine to one. Four years later, Republican Hoover's promise of "a chicken in every pot and two cars in every garage" triumphed over the "happy Warrior, Al Smith." Smith was "wet" on the prohibition issue, while Norwell had a long history of being "dry."

It was just eight months into Hoover's term when, in 1929, "Wall Street laid an egg." While Hoover promised that "prosperity was just around the

Appendix

corner," breadlines, soup kitchens and lines of people trying to withdraw funds from failing banks stretched around the corner. In 1932, one of the biggest vote getters in presidential history, Franklin Delano Roosevelt, became the Democratic nominee with his promise of a new Deal for the "forgotten man." Norwell voters, who had supported Hoover in 1928, didn't abandon him, however. Hoover locally polled about four times as many votes as FDR, who won in a national landslide. It seems that Norwell voters agreed that the Depression was part of the normal economic cycle and that too much government interference with the economy should be avoided.

Four years later, Norwell voters gave Republican Alf London almost four times as many votes as Franklin "Deficit" Roosevelt, a surprise in that the vast majority of Norwell citizens were affected, some very seriously, by the lingering Depression. A strong chord of rugged individualism resulted in Norwell's rejected Public Works Authority funds for replacing the high school destroyed by fire in 1935.

The year 1940 found FDR running for an unprecedented third term. FDR argued that he needed a third term to bring the nation completely out of the Depression and for making good on his pledge, "Your sons will not be asked to fight and die in a foreign war." The defense buildup beginning in the summer of 1940 took care of the former and the attack on Pearl Harbor, December 7, 1941, would cancel out the latter. That November, Norwell voters gave their nod to Wendell Wilkie by almost three to one. Many Norwell voters evidently believed that FDR was steering the country into choppy international waters.

In 1944, in the midst of World War II, a dying FDR was elected to a fourth term against New York governor Thomas Dewey. Roosevelt's "Don't change horses in the midst of a stream" had a big countrywide impact, but still he had his weakest Electoral College showing. Norwell voters were close to four to one for Dewey.

On April 12, 1945, Roosevelt died in Warm Springs, Georgia. Harry S. Truman, sworn in as president that evening, presided over V-E Day, made the decision to drop the A-bomb and announced the victory over Japan on August 14, 1945. After the euphoria brought by peace had died down, however, many wondered whether he could meet the challenges of the Soviets and successfully guide the transition to a peacetime economy.

Would the Republican hold over Norwell voters continue? Or would changing postwar demographics and the influx of new residents bring about new election results?

HOW NORWELL VOTED

(Winner in the town of Norwell placed first)

Election	Candidate	Votes
1920	Warren G. Harding (R)	409
	James M. Cox (D)	48
1924	Calvin Coolidge (R)	443
	John W. Davis (D)	48
1928	Herbert Hoover (R)	567
	Alfred E. Smith (D)	122
1932	Herbert Hoover (R)	592
	Franklin D. Roosevelt (D)	153
1936	Alfred M. Landon (R)	672
	Franklin D. Roosevelt (D)	180
1940	Wendell Wilkie (R)	777
	Franklin D. Roosevelt (D)	247
1944	Thomas E. Dewey (R)	808
	Franklin D. Roosevelt (D)	204

CHAPTER 27

PARTY TIME IN NORWELL

1948–2008

Over the past sixty-two years, Americans have gone to the polls to vote
for a president and vice president sixteen times.

The results nationally have been nine Republican winners and seven
Democrats.

Norwell voters, by contrast, have given the nod to the Republican
aspirants fourteen times and to the Democrats twice. But as the decades have
passed, the more than four-to-one margins for Republicans have diminished
to two to one or even less. In 2004, with 5,901 Norwell citizens voting for
president, George W. Bush's plurality was a mere 207 votes. Nevertheless, of
the thirteen towns and two cities covered by the *Patriot Ledger*, only Norwell,
Duxbury and Hanover went for the national victor.

In 1948, with the United States embroiled in a cold war and still faced
with postwar adjustment, a vast majority of Norwell voters endorsed the
aphorism "To err is Truman." All the leading polls had shown Truman
didn't stand a chance against Republican challenger Dewey, whom Alice
Roosevelt Longworth had described as "the little man on the wedding cake."
In this last presidential campaign in which both candidates crisscrossed the
country by rail, "Give 'em Hell, Harry" could later gloat over the political
upset of the century and refer to the erroneous polls as the "sleeping polls."
Might the same be said someday of the exit polls in 2004?

In 1952, Norwell, along with the nation, validated Republican Dwight
Eisenhower's slogan, "I like Ike." Four years later, Norwell and the nation
declared, "I like Ike even better." Not only did Ike not dismantle the best

features of the New Deal, he even surpassed the Democrats in the scope of his highway program. The building of Route 128, along with the construction of the Southeast Expressway and a new Route 3, paved the way for Norwell's later phenomenal population growth.

In 1960, despite favorite son John F. Kennedy heading the Democratic ticket, Norwell accorded Republican Richard Nixon a two-to-one margin. The 1964 Johnson–Goldwater race was the first in the twentieth century in which Norwell voters favored a Democrat. That year, many feared Barry Goldwater's "A choice rather than an echo" slogan was extreme. But soon, the successes of Johnson's Great Society were blocked by the quagmire of Vietnam. A plan to exit Vietnam secured Nixon's election in 1968.

Four years later, Nixon was reelected, winning every state but Massachusetts. Norwell would not gloat two years later, as the rest of the state could, when Nixon became the first president in history to resign the office. Gerald Ford then became the first individual to become president without having been elected either as president or vice president. The provisions of the Twenty-fifth Amendment made this circumstance possible. Unfortunately, his efforts toward healing were soon undermined with the full pardon he granted Nixon for crimes connected with Watergate.

A few phrases and mention of events recall the issues and elections since 1976. Two presidents, Ronald Reagan and William Clinton, have each served two full terms, the first to do so since Eisenhower. There have been three presidential assassination attempts, concerns about inflation and deficits, oil shortages and alternating periods of economic boom and bust. We heard Jimmy Carter speak of a pervasive national malaise and embraced Reagan's call for patriotism and "a new morning in America." We followed a hostage crisis in Iran and a regrettable Iran–Contra scandal. The stirring tearing down of the Berlin Wall was followed closely by the collapse of the Soviet Union. Succeeding years brought the first Gulf War, the war in Afghanistan, the horror of September 11, 2001, and a second invasion of Iraq. The promise shown by "the Man from Hope," with Norwell's endorsing him for a second term, was sadly followed by "Monicagate" and the second presidential impeachment trial in U.S. history. More recently, we have seen a disputed election resolved by the Supreme Court and a subsequent reelection that did not prove to be a mandate.

During the past half century, Norwell has evolved from a relatively isolated enclave of fewer than three thousand people, mostly pursuing agricultural and small industrial pursuits, to a community now numbering more than ten thousand. A great many residents are employed in Boston or in businesses

Appendix

along the Route 128 corridor. The town is recognized as one of the most affluent communities south of Boston, all the while retaining a bygone charm of the quintessential New England town.

In 1948, the population was still largely composed of people of white, Anglo-Saxon, Protestant background, a far cry from the ethnic diversity existing today. Local voting records reveal a trend toward voting according to issues rather than simply following party lines. With all these population, economic and social changes, the virtual Republican monolith of the past no longer exists today.

HOW NORWELL VOTED

(Winner in the town of Norwell placed first)

Election	Candidate	Votes
1948	Thomas E. Dewey (R)	987
	Harry S. Truman (D)	255
1952	Dwight D. Eisenhower (R)	1,284
	Adlai E. Stevenson (D)	294
1956	Dwight D. Eisenhower (R)	1,716
	Adlai E. Stevenson (D)	437
1960	Richard M. Nixon (R)	1,674
	John F. Kennedy (D)	933
1964	Lyndon B. Johnson (D)	1,558
	Barry M. Goldwater (R)	497
1968	Richard M. Nixon (R)	1,717
	Hubert H. Humphrey Jr. (D)	1,390
1972	Richard M. Nixon (R)	2,225
	George S. McGovern (D)	1,624

Election	Candidate	Votes
1976	Gerald R. Ford (R)	2,478
	Jimmy Carter (D)	1,778
1980	Ronald Reagan (R)	2,688
	Jimmy Carter (D)	1,389
1984	Ronald Reagan (R)	3,047
	Walter F. Mondale (D)	1,628
1988	George H. W. Bush (R)	3,068
	Michael S. Dukakis (D)	2,080
1992	George H. W. Bush (R)	2,226
	William J. Clinton (D)	1,956
1996	William J. Clinton (D)	2,523
	Robert J. Dole (R)	2,224
2000	George W. Bush (R)	2,638
	Albert Gore Jr. (D)	2,573
2004	George W. Bush (R)	3,054
	John F. Kerry (D)	2,847
2008	John McCain (R)	3,054
	Barack Obama (D)	2,937

CHRONOLOGY OF NORWELL
HISTORICAL SOCIETY PRESIDENTS

Joseph Foster Merritt (1935–1940)
George C. Turner (1940–1952)
William Gould Vinal (1952-1955)
Margaret Crowell Dumas (1955–1963)
John Hale Chipman (1963–1967)
Quentin Coons (1967–1969)
Richard McMullan (1969–1971)
Richard Leahy (1971–1973)
Joseph Carty (1973–1976)
Jon Bond (1976–1979)
William Garside (1979–1982)
Jeanne Garside (1982–1988)
Grace Carty (1988–1989)

William Slattery (1989–1991)
Sally Medeiros (1991–1994)
Robert Norris (1994–1995)
Gertrude Daneau (1995–1999)
Thomas and Alice Hyslop (1999–2003)
Thomas Hyslop (2003–2004)
Robert Norris (2004–2008)
Wendy Bawabe (2009–present)

SELECTED BIBLIOGRAPHY

BOOKS

Allen, Frederick Lewis. *Only Yesterday*. New York: Bantam Books, 1965.

Amrist, Ralph, ed. *The Confident Years*. New York: American Heritage Publishing Company, n.d.

Bailey, Ruth Chipman. *Where in the World*. Norwell, MA: Clermont Press, 1990.

Bailey, Thomas B. *The American Pageant*. Lexington, MA, and Washington, D.C.: Heath, 1979.

Bendiner, Robert. *Just Around the Corner*. New York: Harper and Row, 1967.

Biographical Review of Plymouth County. Boston: Biographical Review Publishing Co., 1897.

Briggs, L. Vernon. *Shipbuilding on the North River*. Boston: Coburn Brothers, 1889.

Brokaw, Thomas. *The Greatest Generation*. New York: Random House, 1998.

Catton, Bruce. *The Coming Fury*. New York: Doubleday and Company, 1961.

Dos Passos, John. *Mr. Wilson's War*. New York: Doubleday and Company, 1962.

Ellsworth, E.W., J.D. Fiore, Thomas O'Connor and H.T. Oedel. *Massachusetts in the Civil War*. Boston: Massachusetts Civil War Centennial Commission, 1960–1965.

Emerson, George B., Samuel May and Thomas Munford, eds. *Memoirs of Samuel Joseph May*. Boston: Roberts Brothers, 1873.

Garside, Jeanne M., ed. *Historical Homesteads of Norwell, Massachusetts*. Norwell, MA: Norwell Historical Society, 1992.

Garside, Jeanne M. *The Way We Were*. Norwell, MA: Norwell Historical Society, 1992.

Goodwin, Doris Kearns. *No Ordinary Time*. New York: Simon and Schuster, 1995

Halberstam, David. *The Fifties*. New York: Villard Books, 1993.

Lord, Walter. *The Good Years*. New York: Harper and Row, 1960.

MacPherson, James. *Battle Cry of Freedom*. New York: Oxford Press, 1988.

Manchester, William. *The Glory and the Dream—A Narrative History of America, 1932–72*. Boston: Little, Brown, 1973.

Merritt, Joseph Foster. *A Narrative History of South Scituate–Norwell, Mass.* Rockland, MA: Rockland Standard Publishing Company, 1938.

Old Scituate. Boston: Chief Justice Cushing Daughters of the American Revolution, 1921.

Perry, Ruth Winslow. *Norwell Beautiful and A Glimpse of Cape Cod*. Printed in USA, 1977.

———. *Norwell Beautiful No. II*. Printed in the USA, 1985.

Terkel, Stud. *The Good War*. New York: Pantheon Books, 1984.

Turner, George C. *Historia: A Magazine of Local History*. 1899. Rpr., Norwell, MA: Norwell Historical Society, 1988.

Vinal, William G. *Old Scituate Churches in a Changing World*. Norwell, MA: Ladies Alliance of First Parish Church, 1954.

———. *The Rise and Fall of the District School in Plymouth Plantation (1800–1900)*. Norwell, MA: Vinehall Publication, 1958.

PERIODICALS AND PAPERS

Dumas, Margaret Crowell. "Early Days of First Parish," 1964. Paper mimeographed by the Norwell Historical Society, Norwell, MA.

"History of Catholic Church in Norwell." 1980. Paper mimeographed by the Norwell Historical Society, Norwell, MA.

Journal of Members of D. Willard Robinson Post 112 Grand Army of the Republic (1869–1875). Archives of the Norwell Historical Society, Norwell, MA.

Knapp, Mary, and Carol Meshau. "Norwell Schools, 1941–72." Paper mimeographed by the Norwell Historical Society, Norwell, MA.

"Life and Times of William Penn Brooks (1851–1938)." Paper mimeographed by the Norwell Historical Society, Norwell, MA.

Local Censuses of South Scituate, 1850, 1855, 1880. Monographs. Norwell Historical Society Library, Norwell, MA.

Rockland Standard and Plymouth County Advertiser (1874–1934). Microfilm. Rockland Memorial Library, Rockland, MA.

Rockland Standard and Rockland Independent (1934–1963). Microfilm. Rockland Memorial Library, Rockland, MA.

South Scituate/Norwell Town Reports (1850–1963) James Library, Norwell, MA, and the Library of the Norwell Historical Society, Norwell, MA.

"Tour of Jacobs Homestead." Norwell Historical Society. Paper mimeographed by the Norwell Historical Society, Norwell, MA.

United States Census Bureau Data.

Vinal, William Gould. "Churches." Paper mimeographed by the Norwell Historical Society, Norwell, MA.

"Walking Tour of Norwell Village—October 17, 1982." Sponsored by James Library.

,

INDEX

ABOUT THE AUTHOR

A longtime member of the Norwell Historical Society and currently serving on its board of directors, Samuel H. Olson was raised in Rockland, Massachusetts, but has been a resident of Norwell for the past forty years.

He was a 1954 graduate of Bridgewater State Teachers College and received his master of arts degree in history from Boston University in 1957.

Sam Olson taught English, American history and modern European history in the public schools of Abington, Milton and Needham, Massachusetts, for nearly forty years.

Visit us at
www.historypress.net

www.ingramcontent.com/pod-product-compliance
Lightning Source LLC
Chambersburg PA
CBHW060758100426
42813CB00004B/864

* 9 7 8 1 5 4 0 2 2 5 3 3 7 *